Red, White, and

Blueprint for America

A Common Sense Approach
for America's Future

by David Sellar

Red, White, and Blueprint for America

ISBN-13: 978-1453884782

ISBN-10: 1453884785

Table of Contents

Prologue

September 11, 2001

A plane of some sort appears to have crashed into one of the twin towers of the World Trade Center! There is dense, dark smoke billowing from the upper stories of the building! Oh, my God! A second plane has just crashed into the other tower. OH, MY GOD!

I knew then we were at war.

"Let me make this perfectly clear," to borrow a favorite phrase of one of our former famous politicos, this book is based purely on my own personal observations, opinions, perceptions, and speculations. The subject matter discussed in the following chapters reflects subjective, rather than objective criteria. All thoughts expressed herein are the result of what I have listened to on the radio; watched on television; read in the papers, magazines, books, and on websites. If, in the course of reading this book, you happen to take offense with something I have stated, consider it to be taken "out of context," or deem it to be unfair or misrepresentative, I will apologize in advance.

Simply put, I, as the rest of you who have lived through the 2004 and 2008 presidential campaign seasons, have been bombarded with multitudes of information from anybody and everybody with an opinion, regardless of credentials. This has been and is becoming extremely evident by the media coverage during the last election. The media for the most part, despite glaring evidence to the contrary regarding Barack Obama's lack of experience, questionable character, associations with organizations and individuals who were not exactly model citizens, totally abandoned their responsibility to the public as watchdog and advocate of responsible reporting. Because of their hatred of George Bush, the media openly campaigned for Obama and gave him a free pass on everything. There is credible rumor that *The New York Times* may even have quashed a story about a possibly illegal association of Obama's campaign to the ACORN organization. How could we trust anything reported by the media? We have been left on our own to cipher through what has been reported just to weed out a modicum of truth

This is simply a story about how and what the average American voter like me is confronted with before making his/her decision about who to cast a vote for on Election Day. I make no pretense about being "Fair and Balanced." I will only vouch for my honesty in conveying to you my own personal observations, opinions, perceptions, speculations, and feelings. If you note a wee bit of sarcasm in the pages that follow, it is purely a result of the campaign process.

Just so you know where my head was at way before I began to write this book, I can tell you that I was "undecided" in 2004, sitting on the fence waiting to be thoroughly convinced who to vote for. That was in 2004. In 2008, I definitely knew for whom to cast my ballot, although I wasn't enthusiastic. Ronald Reagan was the last candidate for whom I enthusiastically cast a vote.

I like to think of myself as a conservative person who is very open minded; hence, my definition of conservative more than likely does not mesh with most political parties' definitions of conservative. I also tend to think that I am fairly representative of most people of my age and sociodemographic. I utterly resent pollsters and the major political parties trying to neatly classify and cubbyhole me with a label. I am an individual, as are all of you.

We each have our own unique desires, moralities, viewpoints, circumstances, and aspirations, all of which shift periodically as our socioeconomic demographics change. Pollsters and party campaign managers should take notice: DO NOT TAKE US FOR GRANTED!

This is my story.

Chapter 1

When Time Had No Meaning

I feel it necessary to first establish my credentials by way of a timeline. In doing so, it will become evident (I hope) to all who read this where I came from and how I arrived where I am now.

My father was a veteran of the Big One, World War II. He served in the Pacific theater as a medic, although I cannot be certain, as he would never speak freely about the war. After the war, my parents bought a Levitt house in Westbury, New York, a suburb of New York City in the county of Nassau on Long Island. Our home, one in a development of 300 just like it, was a no-frills house (kitchen, bathroom, living room, two bedrooms, and an unfinished attic) on an eighth of an acre. By today's standards, the house would be considered tiny, a starter house. Back then it was a castle. The development had previously been pastureland for a local dairy farm. Someone once told me that there was a horse-drawn fire engine stationed on the next block over, where we fed horses carrots. I have no recollection of this, being but a tiny tot, but assume it to be true, as the area back then was pretty rural. Whenever relatives or friends of the family came out from the city to visit, they always questioned my parents as to why they chose to live all the way out at the end of the earth.

I arrived on the scene in 1953 amidst the rest of the baby boomers. During my early childhood years, I thought there was a law dictating that every family had to have at least three kids, since I didn't know of any in the neighborhood with fewer. What I hadn't realized until later on was that much of the neighborhood was Catholic. I was also born and raised a Catholic. In my earliest days, I couldn't understand why everyone wasn't a Catholic. My parents were deeply religious, and, as a result when I reached school age, I was enrolled in the local Catholic elementary school. I was extremely disappointed with this decision, as most of my friends attended the local public school.

The nuns taught better than 90% of the classes and scared the living daylights out of me. There were minimally 40 children in a class, and silence among other things was golden. No one even dreamed of talking, or for that matter uttering a whisper in class, for the odds of getting caught were better than 100 to 1. The consequences for getting caught ranged from standing out in the hall, banishment from the classroom, a trip to the principal's office, an all-night writing assignment for homework to punishments of a more corporal nature. These were dished out with impunity for any perceived offense, rightly or wrongly deserved.

As terrifying as this was during school hours, what waited at home when your parents found out was enough to make you consider running away. In my parents' eyes, there was no such thing as a trial by jury. The nuns were judge, jury, and executioner. Needless to say, I was always on my best behavior, but, nonetheless, I endured my fair share of misfortunes (bleeding knuckles, involuntary donations to the missions, etc.), and eight years of Catholic elementary schooling was, to say the least, a terrifying and memorable experience. Once I was old enough, at my parents' urging, I became an altar boy. I found myself each weekday morning, no matter the weather, peddling my bicycle five miles to church to serve 6:30 a.m. mass.

I was the youngest of three, with two older brothers. Some of my fondest memories were of spinning my oldest brother's collection of 45s, 33 LPs, and an occasional 78 on the Victrola. Perry Como, Chubby Checker, and Bobby Darin were followed by my other brother's favorites: the Beach Boys, the Brothers Four, and the Mamas and the Papas.

Father Knows Best, Ozzie and Harriet, and *Leave It to Beaver* exemplified my family life. *The Wonder Years,* a more recent, nostalgic TV series, was a fairly accurate depiction of my childhood. Back in those days, there was no such thing as a computer or the internet. Our free time, unlike that of today's kids, was spent outdoors playing with friends and using our imagination to act out innumerable roles of play. We also spent quite a bit of time reading books. My favorites were *The Hardy Boys* detective series, biographies of famous people, and stories about historical events. My prize possession, however, was *The American Heritage* series, 24 volumes that chronicled our nation's history. They were purchased when I was somewhere around the age of ten at the local supermarket. Every two weeks over the course of a year, a new volume would become available. I spent untold hours reading and rereading these until I could almost recite them from memory.

Saturday nights were reserved for television and pinochle. I sat with my father and watched the New York Rangers hockey games (I'm a diehard Islanders fan now). Even though the Rangers could never win the Stanley Cup, we never gave up hope. After the hockey game, neighbors would arrive and my parents would play pinochle for hours. My father was a master player, and I watched and absorbed everything I could, waiting for the day when I would be invited to play. Sunday nights we were allowed to watch *The Wonderful World of Disney* on television, and, as we got older, to stay up to watch *Bonanza*.

My father left for work every morning around 6:30 a.m., wearing his suit, necktie, overcoat, and felt hat, indistinguishable from the thousands of other commuters on the Long Island Railroad on their daily trek into New York City. He arrived home like clockwork (railroad permitting), at 6 p.m., and dinner was served at 6:15 p.m. sharp. The menu was usually some variant of beef with boiled potatoes, a boiled green vegetable, and if we were really lucky maybe niblet corn. Being

Catholic, Fridays was fish sticks. Tomato sauce consisted of ketchup, and salt was the only seasoning known to the household. Simply put, my mother, God bless her soul, was a terrible cook.

My first introduction to politics was of the office variety. My father would hold court at the dinner table and give my mother a detailed, blow-by-blow description of what transpired during his day. I was fascinated and absorbed it all. By dessert, the conversation shifted from office politics to church politics. My father was a convert to Catholicism, and both he and my Mother at one time or another belonged to, or ran, every organization and function in the parish. Needless to say, I was always volunteered to help out.

My typical Sundays consisted of selling raffle tickets in front of the church from before 6:30 a.m. mass to after 1:00 p.m. mass. Looking back, I can easily equate the church building fund deficit to the federal deficit. It never seemed to go away either, despite all the hard work and good intentions. Both of my brothers being older than me always seemed able to escape these weekly rituals. The one positive derived from these weekly conscriptions was the tremendous amount of time I was able to spend with my father as I grew up.

My father was a simple man. He never went to college. I, to this day, am not even sure that he finished high school. He immigrated to this country from Scotland when he was a small child. As a child, I was always taught to listen and only speak when spoken to. As a result of listening, I learned over the years that my father grew up in New York, spending much of his childhood on Staten Island. He often spoke of working either with a pushcart, or delivering milk during his youth. I do not recall ever hearing him speak of good times during his childhood. The only fun he ever revealed was just before and immediately after the war, when family and friends from the old neighborhood got together to go bowling or play poker.

What I did learn about my father was how hard working and honest an individual he was. One night on the walk home from the train station, he found a packet that contained bearer bonds, the amount of which was a veritable fortune. He somehow was able to trace down the rightful owner who was extremely appreciative of my father's honesty and rewarded him with $50, which I gather was the equivalent of about a week's pay. My father never complained about his situation in life, and instead volunteered his time and energy for the betterment of others. He rarely raised his voice to either me or my brothers, and I can hardly ever recall him being mad. He, like most parents of that era, simply dedicated his life to ensuring that his children were afforded the opportunity to attend college and have a future that would be better than his was.

My mother was the typical June Cleaver/Harriet Nelson from the *Leave It to Beaver/Father Knows Best* era. She kept the house, washed the clothes and hung them out to dry in the backyard, ironed everything, darned the socks, sewed on buttons, and put patches on the knees of our dungarees. She walked to the store every day to do the grocery shopping (with her collection of cents-off coupons), cooked our meals, and checked our homework. On Saturday nights, she relaxed while watching the Champagne music of Lawrence Welk on TV.

From as far back as I can remember I delivered newspapers. Each of my brothers had their own route. My oldest brother delivered *The Long Island Press*, and my other brother delivered *Newsday*. As soon as they would get home from school, we loaded up the bicycles and for the next couple of hours trudged through the neighborhood. We would usually finish up by 4:30 p.m. or 5:00 p.m. Fridays were collection day, which meant finishing up around 7:00 p.m. I hated rainy days when everything ended up soggy, and snowy days when we substituted sleighs for bicycles. I particularly remember Fridays when collecting. The paper cost 30¢ for the week, and about half the customers gave us a 5¢ tip. One customer would always give me a 10¢ tip and tell me to buy a boat, a car or an airplane, and one person would always give me a 20¢ tip.

In the winter we shoveled snow and during the summer we cut lawns for extra cash that was always saved for our education. As my brothers got older, I inherited the paper routes, and as soon as I was old enough to get working papers, I moved on to the local supermarket, where I worked every hour possible until I graduated from college.

When I graduated from elementary school, I applied to and was accepted by St. Mary's in Manhasset, New York. I worked every day after school in the supermarket to pay for tuition. When I graduated high school, I moved on to Manhattan College in Riverdale, New York. I worked in the supermarket every weekend and in a flight kitchen at LaGuardia airport during summer vacations to cover tuition. By my sophomore year in college, I had saved enough to purchase my first car. It was a beauty, a brand new 1973 Chevy Vega hatchback. It was a three-speed, four-cylinder, aluminum-block engine (that hadn't warped). I had the car all of a year and a half, when, one night while the car was parked in front of my house, some drunk plowed into it and totaled it. I was heartbroken. What the insurance paid wasn't nearly enough to replace it.

My college years fell smack in the middle of a political sideshow called the Vietnam War. Actually it had been building rapidly throughout my high school years and culminated during college. All during high school, the war was only on the periphery for me. Social disobedience, campus unrest, protests, and draft dodgers seemed to go hand in hand with flower power, free love, drugs, and music. Woodstock was where it was at, but I really did not completely comprehend the motivating factors for it until my later years in college.

Reality hit home during my junior year with the draft lottery. I ended up with a number somewhere in the middle of the pack, but still knew that as soon as I graduated, I would be winning an all-expenses-paid trip to Vietnam, courtesy of Uncle Sam. I really didn't know what Nam was all about, but I was an American and knew my responsibility was to serve my country when called upon. I was probably the only student on campus to have an American flag hanging on the wall of my dorm room, and still believed in what it stood for. Luckily for me and countless others, the war ended before it engulfed me. It was, however, the beginning of my growing interest in government and politics. Richard Millhouse Nixon provided much reading material and an awakening of sorts.

Upon graduation from college, armed with a B.S. degree in marketing and economics (double major), I began my adult working life as a store-level assistant manager trainee with Korvettes, in the small appliances and giftware departments. I passed up multiple excellent opportunities with previous employers (for which I have continually kicked myself, hindsight being 20/20), because I wanted more than anything to be a buyer. In less than a year, I worked my way into the corporate buying office where I held multiple positions, making my way up the ladder to that buyer title. My dream come true evaporated with the "Other Korvettes" advertising campaign. The company tried to reposition itself from a very successful mass merchant discounter of hard goods to an upscale department store selling designer jeans and high fashion soft goods. Within six months, Korvettes folded. I was lucky, as a vendor of mine hired me to be a regional sales manager of housewares. I lasted all of a year. Sales was definitely not my calling.

I took the next year off, more or less dropped out of the white-collar work force while desperately trying to identify my niche in corporate society. A friend of mine owned an auto dismantling business and offered me a job driving a delivery truck until I figured out what I wanted to do when I grew up. Working in a junkyard for a year provided the motivation to rejoin the real world. While the work was honest as the day was long, it was a long day. Six days a week, minimum pay, no paid vacations, no paid days off and no benefits to speak of, but it was a job. I worked with some truly amazing people and was introduced to some of the most unsavory characters and destinations imaginable.

On Sundays, I scoured *The New York Times* employment section, trying to find something more to my liking and ability. Every Sunday, the employment section was filled with at least four full pages of employment opportunities for computer programmers. While in college, I had learned to program and was actually quite good at it. It never dawned on me that I could make a living doing something that came so naturally to me, and was both challenging and fun to do. The only problem was that I didn't know any of the programming languages that were required for the open positions. Lo and behold, there was a school nearby that offered an intense training program in a condensed time period.

I scraped together every last penny I could, enrolled in the next session and said a fond farewell to my noble flatbed delivery truck. School was a full-time proposition between class work and studying. It was also a fiscal drain on my bank account, which had dwindled to nearly nothing. Problem solved! I went to school during the day and pumped gas at an all-night station. It didn't pay much, but it fit my schedule. By the time I finished school, I had $23 left to my name and no way to pay next month's rent.

I envisioned the halls of school lined with recruiters waiting with offers the day we graduated. Wrong! What I hadn't counted on was something called experience, or lack thereof. What I now faced was a Catch-22. There were literally thousands of jobs available for programmers with over two years of experience, but none for programmers without experience. The magic phrase "entry level" was akin to "bubonic plague."

Since I had the classic "funds-are-low" disease, in desperation, I took a job with a mom-and-pop gourmet grocery store delivering orders to the local rich and famous. It actually turned out pretty well as the base pay was livable, the tips excellent and all the day-old fish and produce I could carry home was free. The owner knew when he hired me that I was transitioning to other work, and if I was willing to work Saturdays, he was willing to let me have Wednesdays off to find another job.

I spent the better part of six months pounding the Manhattan pavement, knocking on doors and filling out endless employment applications in search of that entry-level position. Eventually, I was granted an interview with a well-known retailer. Much to their credit, they at least recognized talent when they saw it! The whole truth was that during the interview, my prospective employer asked about a previous job I had on my resume. He couldn't quite grasp why I wanted to change careers to become a programmer and leave a position as an "energy transfer engineer" specializing in the distribution of hydrocarbon chain based fuels. With a straight face, I simply stated, "I was tired of pumping gas." He stared at me with a quizzical look on his face and asked, "When can you start?" I've since learned that programmers are a strange lot.

The following 23 years have been spent plying that trade on behalf of retailers, healthcare insurers, distributors, software developers and wholesalers. I have worked on the design, development and implementation of point of sale, warehousing/distribution, claims payment, medical disease classification, mortality, medical analysis, statistical analysis, modeling and videotape management systems. I have coded in many different languages and built untold numbers of databases.

I have lived through both good and not so good economic times. I have ridden an emotional rollercoaster for many years. Some high times were when I got married and the birth of my daughter. Some lows were the deaths of my parents and that of my wife after a very long terminal illness. I have championed structured religion and then walked away in disgust. I have volunteered my time and energy freely to both church and community. I have never forgotten from whence I came, and for all intents and purposes, I believe that I am representative of most Americans, for I am you, and you are me.

On the political front, I was discouraged by Nixon's Watergate scandal and felt helpless and downtrodden by Carter's ineptitude and inability to successfully resolve the Iran hostage crisis. My spirit had been lifted by Reagan's leadership and his dismantling of the Evil Empire; I was proud to be an American while Bush orchestrated Desert Storm, disappointed by Clinton's leadership and antics, terrified of Al Gore (Mr. "I invented the internet") and indifferent to "Dubbya" (the lesser of two evils). For me, politics was just a necessary evil and a sideshow at that. That all changed for me on the bright clear autumn New York morning of September 11, 2001.

Throughout our young nation's history there have been a number of hallmark events that served to galvanize the population with steadfast resolve and transform indifference to action. In the beginning there were Concord and Lexington, Bunker Hill and Paul Revere's famous ride which heralded the birth of our nation. Other such events that come to mind are the sinking of the Maine in Havana harbor; the firing on Fort Sumter to initiate the Civil War; the sinking of the Lusitania, which helped pave our entry into World War I; and the attack on Pearl Harbor, which engulfed us in World War II. For most of us, these events are but points on our nation's timeline of historical events. But for an ever-dwindling population of veterans, there is little or no emotional attachment to any of these events. September 11, 2001, now commonly referred to as 9/11, is another hallmark event that shook the bedrock of America. It was this generation's Pearl Harbor.

I can still vividly recall that morning, pulling into the parking lot at work and listening to the radio, transfixed, staring at the car radio as if it were a television. The first reports I had heard were from Tom Kaminsky, a helicopter traffic reporter for News Radio 88. He reported that it appeared a small plane had crashed into one of the World Trade Center towers, and smoke was billowing from the building. When he said that he would attempt to fly over there to get a better look, I went inside to work.

I, along with coworkers, gathered around a computer, watching CNN's website for more info, and listened to the radio for any additional information. At this point, no one had any inclination to believe that this was anything but an unbelievably horrible accident. Based upon the pictures we saw of the tower, we began to speculate about the size of the plane that hit the building. A few minutes later, there was no longer any need to speculate. A second plane, a commercial airliner, slammed into the other tower. It took all of about two seconds for the realization to hit home that this was definitely orchestrated and we were under some sort of attack. After the better part of a few hours, facts were gathered and analyzed; many rumors were dispelled; and theories, many incomplete but fairly conclusive, began to emerge.

My commute to work takes me through New York City, and reports of the bridges and tunnels being closed for emergency purposes required me to find an alternate way home that day. I was lucky enough to leave work early and secure a spot on the Port Jefferson ferry that crossed Long Island Sound from Bridgeport, Connecticut, to Long Island. While on the ferry, many people just sat, totally in shock, and watched the television coverage of the towers collapsing. Out on deck as we crossed the sound, looking west toward New York City, a tremendous dark cloud of smoke was visible rising from downtown Manhattan. There almost appeared to be an air of disbelief as everyone digested and contemplated what had happened.

For me, not having been directly targeted by the attacks, the impact of the enormity of what happened only gradually began to take shape. I was focused on the television coverage continuously for at least ten hours, hoping to discover the entire extent of the attack. Whether real or imagined, I continuously heard the sound of jets flying along the coastline that evening. With each occurrence, I would run outside and look skyward, hoping to allay my fears of what might be happening again. Over the next several days, as more tidbits of information were pieced together and the callousness of the attacks sank in, my outrage climbed ever higher. I wanted so badly to hit back at these sons of bitches with all my might, yet felt powerless to do so. The decision to attack Afghanistan only partially sated my anger and thirst for revenge.

The days immediately following the attack turned out to be an emotional rollercoaster for me. Living where I do had a lot to do with this. The World Trade Center was in my backyard, so to speak. The many years when I worked in Manhattan caused me to be in the twin towers for a whole host of reasons on countless occasions. There was a personal connection between those towers and me. Each morning, for many days afterwards, as I drove to work, heading west on Ocean Parkway along Jones Beach, from 30 miles away I could still see that tremendous dark cloud of smoke rising from downtown Manhattan. It seemed that everyone in the New York metropolitan area had some sort of connection with the tragedy, either personally knowing someone who worked at the towers, was killed or missing, was a firefighter, or was an emergency services person or volunteer who helped out in some way or another on the "pile."

One of the strongest emotions that I felt almost immediately was that of patriotism, both as an American and as a New Yorker. It became very apparent, very quickly, that what had happened had affected almost everyone simultaneously and to a tremendous degree. On my drive home from work, on Ocean Parkway there was an abandoned building with a very tall flagpole. Attached to the flagpole was an enormous American flag that had slid down the pole and came to rest in a tangled, battered mess on the rooftop. I hadn't really noticed it before, but I did then, and it made my blood boil. Apparently it bothered two other people as well. I pulled into the parking lot where the three of us in an unspoken agreement, climbed up to the roof of the building, untangled and hoisted the flag. The three of us in unison stepped back, looked up at the now fluttering American flag and silently saluted. To this day, whenever there is an American flag ceremony being performed, it brings a tear to my eye.

It is often said that Rome has some of the craziest drivers, resulting in some of the worst driving conditions imaginable. One only has to drive anywhere in the New York metro area during rush hour to know that Rome doesn't come close to the absolute madness experienced here on a daily basis. The term *road rage* almost definitely emanated from New York. Immediately after 9/11, American flags began to appear on almost every vehicle on the road. There was a feeling of unity that was unprecedented in my lifetime. It seemed that random acts of kindness totally replaced the typical indifference that was heretofore commonplace. As strange as it may seem, almost every driver exhibited and extended courtesies to other drivers. 9/11 had a major impact on all Americans, New Yorkers and especially me! There was now a new focal point for our collective rage.

I will be the first to admit that before 9/11 I really had not paid that much attention to the so-called terrorist threat. My awareness of terrorism was principally focused on Israel and the Palestinians. I considered myself to be fairly well-informed — that is to say, I listened to the news on the radio for a minimum of three hours a day while driving to and from work and felt I was up to speed on current events. In hindsight, I guess you could say that I listened to the news, but didn't really hear it.

I was still working in Manhattan when the first World Trade Center bombing occurred, but never attributed it to a very well-organized and orchestrated group of terrorists. While the bombing made headlines, it wasn't something that made me sit up and take notice; rather it was just another event in an average New York day. After all, it wasn't something that happened on the block where I worked — it was all the way downtown. When the United States embassies in Africa were bombed, again it seemed distant. Granted, they were coordinated or connected, but it was half a world away, and easily dismissed as just another splinter group run amuck. The world seemed to be in almost constant conflict. Somalia; the USS Cole; the bombing of the Alfred P. Murrah Federal Building in Oklahoma City; the marine barracks car bombing in Beirut; the IRA terrorism in London and Northern Ireland; the Russians in Afghanistan; Serbia and Croatia; Desert Storm; Iran and Iraq; the almost daily incidents between Israel and the Palestinians. It was all so far away, so constant, and so impersonal for so many of us. If it didn't disrupt our daily lives, then it didn't even appear on our radar screen. Well, that all changed on September 11, 2001, and I began to take things a bit more personally.

Chapter 2

The Presidential Derby

"It has been said that politics is the second oldest profession. I have learned that it bears a striking resemblance to the first."
—Ronald Reagan

Here is what I predicted the outcomes of the 2004 party primaries and the national election would be. I predicted that George Bush would win the Republican nomination, but that Dick Cheney would drop off the ticket with health problems, replaced by John McCain. Joseph Lieberman with John Edwards would be the Democratic ticket. The presidential election would be won by Bush 57 % to Lieberman's 40 %, with Nader garnering 3% to 4 % of the vote.

Now that you see how well I can predict, I will not bore you with my thoughts regarding the 2008 results. They are just as accurate.

From the standpoint of our country's welfare, it does not really matter who ends up winning elections. What does matter is that all elected officials work together for the betterment of our country. No doubt, there will always be differences in opinion, but the will of the people MUST take precedence over partisan politics. We must never forget: United We Stand, Divided We Fall. I always bear in mind that the last two elections have been extremely close, especially when the vote is defined by the popular vote as opposed to the electoral vote. In either election, there has not been a mandate for the victorious party by the popular vote. The country has been very evenly split as to choice of party. This in turn means that the victorious party MUST seek to govern in a bipartisan spirit in order to answer to the will of the people. There can be no exclusion of the losing party.

I am very disappointed in President Obama. Despite all his campaign rhetoric and promises to implement change with a governing style that would include ALL elected officials in a bipartisan fashion, he utterly failed his first test within three weeks of taking office. At an early Democrat caucus in Virginia, he played to his Democrat compatriots and ridiculed Republicans regarding the stimulus package. During the time of formulation and debate of this package, both he and Nancy Pelosi in no uncertain terms let the Republicans know that the Democrats won the election and the Republican legislators should bend to the will of the victor.

This is not only foolish, but dangerous. This is clearly evidenced by the overwhelming disapproval rating garnered for the House stimulus package crafted solely by the Democrats and forced upon the Republicans. The majority of the populace (Democrats and Republicans) didn't see it the same way as the Democrat legislators and Obama. Not a single Republican voted in favor of this bill. If this is an example of things to come, we as a country are in for an extremely turbulent four years of partisan politics. I will also venture to predict that the Democrats will once again snatch defeat from the jaws of victory if they disregard the will of the people while pursuing their own personal agendas. I truly hope this is not the case, as I put the welfare of my country above my own personal agenda.

Chapter 3

What's Wrong?

"If ever a time should come, when vain and aspiring men shall possess the highest seats in Government, our country will stand in need of its experienced patriots to prevent its ruin."

—Samuel Adams

How many of you remember the 1980 Winter Olympics at Lake Placid, New York? How many of you remember the semifinal round of the hockey series? How many of you watched the U.S. vs. U.S.S.R. game on television? Do you remember what it felt like when the game ended and the United States Olympic Hockey Team, comprised of college hockey players, beat the U.S.S.R. team, comprised of the best professional hockey players that the Soviets had to offer? Do you remember the euphoric pride you felt?

The last time that things were remotely good about this country was when the citizens actually felt a sense of pride similar to the 1980 Olympic hockey win. In my judgment that equated to Ronald Reagan's presidency and a brief period after the 9/11 tragedy. We were unquestionably a united country.

Since then, we have been on a continuous and seemingly irreversible downhill slide. The contributing factors are so numerous that to list them all would require an entire book. Hang on to your hats, my fellow Americans, because I'm going to tell you the primary reason for our sorry state of affairs. Are you ready?

Politicians: AKA *Stuffed Shirts & Empty Suits*

Yup, you guessed it, boys and girls, our own beloved elected officials. As of a recent poll in 2009, the collective approval rating for Congress was an astounding 25%. Even lawyers and used car salesmen get a higher rating. How can this be, you may ask?

Simply put, our elected officials have forgotten why they were sent to Washington, D.C. They forgot that they were sent on our behalf to do our bidding. They have forgotten that we are their employers. They have forgotten that they are beholden and answerable to each of us, JOE and JANE CITIZEN.

Ever write to one of your elected officials to voice your concern about something? I have many times. I wrote to Hillary Clinton when she was a senator, and never got an acknowledgement from either her or one of her flunkies. I guess her mail was not forwarded to her while she conducted her own personal business (i.e., campaigning for president) out of state on our time and on our dime. (Before I get too far off track, see more on this issue in Chapter 4, Campaign Reform.). Do our voices as constituents really count for anything once a candidate has been elected to office?

Way back in the early days of our country, Thomas Jefferson and John Adams held opposing beliefs regarding just who should run the country, and who should be allowed to vote. Jefferson believed that only landowners should be allowed to vote and only the educated wealthy should hold office. He did not give much credence to the abilities of the uneducated to elect officials capable of running our government.

John Adams believed that the common man was more than capable of self-determination. (At this point, I will assign some homework. Please read Tom Clancy's *Executive Orders*. While the story is fictional, there is a lot of truth in his writing. I do not know if he intended to convey a subtle message in this novel, but his portrayal of President Ryan and his way of thinking regarding service to his nation sure hit a home run with me.)

Today, generally speaking, every American citizen who reaches the age of 18, regardless of intellect or wealth, has the right to vote. In some ways both Jefferson and Adams have won. Everyone can vote, provided they are motivated or care enough to register and go to the polls on Election Day. Sadly, only a small percentage of voting-age citizens take this privilege and responsibility seriously enough to vote.

Maybe the reason that so few people vote anymore is because the overall populace has become so disconnected, disillusioned and disgusted with the choice of candidates that they have become disinterested. Campaigns, and hence elections, have become a sideshow of negativity with attack advertisements ever more predominant as Election Day approaches. Instead of addressing the legitimate concerns of our country, the elections have become a game of polarization with one party diametrically opposed to the other. The political views and values of the extreme spectrums of the two major parties have become the dominant issues of the elections.

In actuality, these positions probably are of little interest to the vast majority of the population. The issues are typically hyped to such an extent as to divide the country along party lines, when in reality most people couldn't care less. It is no wonder that *American Idol*, Lindsay Lohan, Britney Spears, and Paris Hilton are topics of greater interest than government policies fabricated to serve politicians only.

It's also no wonder that the rest of the world looks at us with amazement and fails to take us seriously, or, more important, with utter disdain! Our politics are so fractured that we have become a splintered nation that should be renamed the "Divisive States of America." The unity of value and purpose is gone.

The tail wags the dog!

To illustrate, think back to your days in high school or college when you took statistics. Remember the bell curve, so named because the shape of the statistical curve resembled that of a bell? Do you remember what a "normal distribution" was? For those of you having trouble reaching back that far, a normal distribution is simply a grouping of values from a population. When taking a random sample of a population, based upon a specific value, typically the resulting distribution will reflect half the population on the right side of a midpoint, and half on the left. The bell curve would be symmetrical in shape. Say you were asked, "On a scale of 1 to 10 how would you rate your feelings: 1 being not much interest and 10 being extremely passionate?" The largest number of people respond with a rating of 5 or 6, a smaller total would respond with a 4 or 7, an even lesser number would respond with a 3 or 8, fewer would respond with a 2 or 9, and finally the least amount of people would respond with a 1 or 10. Of those who responded, 90% would be between 2 and 9, 80% between 3 and 8, and 60% between 4 and 7. The extremes 1 and 10, and to a lesser degree 2 and 9, are considered outliers and represent little significance. Yet, these outliers are the driving forces that have shaped our recent party politics. The more extreme you can be, the better you'll be able to differentiate yourself from your opponent. Hence the tail, 10% of the populace wags the dog, or 90% of the populace. We are divided by the extremes, polarized by the media, and paralyzed by our inability to effect meaningful change.

The phrase "United we stand, divided we fall" has taken on a relevance and urgency all its own. It is why I have undertaken the task of writing this book. I am not a naturally gifted writer, as you can probably tell by now. My motivation stems purely from patriotism. We ARE the greatest country in the world, and if we don't wake up to the fact that we are becoming more and more divided each day, we will soon be referred to as WAS the greatest country in the world. Our preoccupation and rabid indulgence in internal petty politics has torn the fabric of this nation to pieces and blinded us to the most serious issues that this country has faced in many a year.

As I stated earlier, my wake-up call was 9/11, and since then I have witnessed a seemingly irreversible downhill slide. I hope that this book will serve as a wake-up call to at least some of you. I have become disgusted with the bias of the media in their reporting, the ineptitude of our elected officials to address and resolve strategic issues, the overall decline of our moral values, and the decline of our stature in the eyes of the world. It is time to hold our elected officials accountable to the needs and desires of our nation, and remind them of just whom they work for.

Instead of letting the Republicans and Democrats define what the major issues are, we need to speak up and define the issues ourselves. We should press candidates to unequivocally state their views on sensitive issues. We should challenge all candidates at every level to produce a thorough, well-thought-out platform that benefits the bulk of the citizens, not just the fringes. Every candidate should be espousing a platform that strengthens America, and commit to the betterment of citizens. Platitudes and catch phrases don't count; well-defined initiatives accompanied by reasonably attainable goals and strategies to achieve them are what make a difference. Let me give you a few examples.

The following is pasted from the February 25, 2008, CNN website. It is a timely example demonstrating my issue with politicians. Hillary Clinton, while campaigning for the Democratic Party presidential nomination, is legitimate in her accusation of people desiring action rather than just words. However, she is, at the same time, guilty of exactly the same thing.[1]

Meantime, in response to a question regarding immigration during a Spanish language television debate, Hillary tells the audience that certain people (namely Lou Dobbs of CNN) are basically anti-Latino immigrant. I have been listening to Lou Dobbs crusade against illegal immigrants for over a year. He is not anti-Latino immigration; he is against illegals that come across the border from Mexico illegally. Hillary surely knew the difference between legal and illegal immigration, yet she conscientiously chose to sidestep the real issue and pander to the Latino community, clearly demonstrating her lack of backbone and integrity. Hillary had the opportunity to take a stand and propose an honest solution to the illegal immigration problem we have with Mexico. Instead she chose to point the finger at someone who IS addressing the problem, portraying Lou Dobbs as the villain, all the while preserving the ability to talk out of all sides of her mouth without committing to anything.

We cannot allow politicians to get away with pandering to a specific special interest group one day, and say the opposite the next day to a different special interest group. We must hold them to their word.

You and only you hold the key to putting this country back on track. You alone need to register to vote, learn about the candidates, voice your opinions to the media and the candidates, and challenge all candidates at every level to produce a thorough, well-thought-out platform that benefits all citizens. Do not let the candidates just criticize one another. Demand detailed solutions to meaningful issues, hold them to their stated positions, get involved, and most importantly, on Election Day, VOTE!

In the following chapters, I have laid out issues that I feel are of the utmost importance to the survival of this nation. I have in some cases put forth some of my own thoughts on how to deal with these issues.

You may not agree, but at least I am putting something akin to a platform out there for all to see. If it stirs debate or raises awareness of the dire straits we are in, then I believe I have achieved something. The collective blowhards that run our country on our behalf don't seem to have a clue, and neither did most of the potential candidates for the presidency.

EXTRA...EXTRA...EXTRA....Used Car Salesmen Have More Creditability Than Politicians!

Congress had the lowest all-time approval rating in 2008 (at one point I thought I had read it was down to 14% and seemingly dropping by the minute, inverse to the price of oil). Not only is this pitiful, but it is also unforgivable.

Our collection of potential candidates for the presidential nomination of 2008 were all beating the same drum. They took pot shots at each other and dealt with the "hot topics" de jour. I have followed them and their commentary, speeches, etc. and come away extremely disappointed. I have heard few original thoughts escape their collective mouths regarding future vision. All of them were too busy defending their previous records (most of which needed defending), spinning their gibberish, speaking out of both sides of their mouths, and not really taking a stand on anything that really matters.

This needs to change and now![2]

It seems that most elected officials care only about getting reelected, and to do that, they need to take the path that gets them the most recognition and campaign donations (do I sound cynical?), even if it deliberately flies in the face of what the citizens whom they represent actually want. It is time to clean house. We need elected officials who fill up their own gas tanks, buy their own gallons of milk and loaves of bread. We need elected officials who worry about how they will be able to pay their taxes when they are due (some of Obama's choices for cabinet positions seemed to have trouble meeting that obligation). We need regular Janes and Joes who are in touch with reality and actually work for a living, not a bunch of star struck actors whose only interest is advancement of their own career at our expense.

I wish both Hillary Clinton and John McCain had the integrity to resign from the Senate when they decided to run for president. Everyone knows that Hillary started campaigning even prior to her reelection to a second term as U.S. Senator from New York. Their entire focus had been on campaigning to get elected, forgetting that they were already elected to a job that I feel they had utterly neglected. This sentiment applies to all candidates who currently hold public office. One of the most offensive phrases that I hear constantly bandied about is, "the powerful chairman of the such and such committee." This phrase always refers to an elected politician. I find it extremely offensive because as an elected official, this person's authority is derived from the constituents that elected him to serve them. He is no more powerful than any other person elected to public office. Who are these "powerful" politicians? How did they become so powerful? More often than not, the answer to these questions can be found by identifying the politicians who have been serving in their elected positions longer than their colleagues. When politicians accumulate so much power they become dictatorial. "We the people" are shortchanged, and become insignificant and subservient to the personal desires and ambitions of a few. Common sense would dictate that the best way to protect "We the People" from the possible abuses of "powerful" politicians is to mandate term limits. The office of the president is constitutionally limited to two terms for these reasons and others. I believe that all elected offices should be term limited.

Politicians: aka Stuffed Shirts & Empty Suits — that's what's WRONG!

Notes.

1. Taking a mocking swipe at the Illinois senator's (Barack Obama) campaign style, Clinton said people want actions and not words. "I could stand up here and say 'Let's just get everybody together, let's get unified, the sky will open, the light will come down, celestial choirs will be singing and everyone will know we should do the right thing and the world will be perfect,'" she said Sunday while campaigning in Providence, Rhode Island.

2. To illustrate just what I mean, here is a piece that I read on the CNN website the other day. The quote is from Barack Obama regarding just how insane the process of running for president is. This is what he said to Jon Stewart on Comedy Central's *The Daily Show*.

"So we're preparing and one of my staff said, 'The thing you've got to understand is, this isn't on the level.' And I think that really strikes to what people are frustrated with in politics, is that so much of what we talk about, so much of what we say, it's not true, people know it's not true, all the insiders understand that we're just game-playing — and in the meantime you've got these hugely serious problems, which are true."

Thanks for the illumination. Instead of a presidential election, why don't we just hold a beauty pageant instead! In the words of Donald Rumsfeld, "There are things we know, and things we don't know ...."

Talk about hugely serious problems, here is another example of why career politicians no longer have our trust and confidence, and hence, shouldn't be running our country. The following was reported by CNN on their website on 5/31/07.

WASHINGTON (AP) Democratic presidential candidate John Edwards misspoke when he said he read a National Intelligence Report before authorizing the war in Iraq, his campaign said.

Edwards did not read the classified report that contained doubts about the existence of weapons of mass destruction in Iraq, his spokesman said, even though it was available to him at the time when he was a North Carolina senator serving on the Intelligence Committee.

Edwards spokesman Eric Schultz said Edwards had read the declassified summary report before voting to authorize the war, but not the full version.

However, when asked Wednesday whether he read the confidential report, Edwards told employees at Google, "I read it."

Schultz said Friday that Edwards "simply misunderstood the question."

"As Senator Edwards has said many times before, he read the declassified version of the NIE, as well as other intelligence documents, which were ultimately summarized in the classified version of the NIE," Schultz said.

Edwards's chief rival, New York Sen. Hillary Rodham Clinton, acknowledged this week that she also did not read the full report before voting to authorize the war. Reported by CNN 5/31/07.

This report was made available to all senators and congresspersons before any vote to authorize the war in Iraq was taken. We also know that in order to read this document, all who entered the room where it was available were required to sign a register. Well, guess what? Only a tiny amount of our elected officials ever took the opportunity to read this document. Maybe all the questions regarding the assumptions made in the intelligence reports would have been questioned before the vote instead of after the war began if our elected officials found the time to research such a monumental vote. After all, isn't this what we elect them to do and pay them for? I guess it's easier to just blame Bush and the intelligence services for this major screw up. I am not necessarily picking on the aforementioned personalities, but they are campaigning for the presidency. If they cannot even do their due diligence in a lesser role, what can we expect of them when they assume the greatest responsibility of any person in the world?

Just in case you forgot, let me remind you: going to war is a very serious action with grave consequences. We know this is so for politicians because of all the back peddling they have done to cover their collective butts as the war has become more and more unpopular.

One last note here, we all know how easy it is to be a Monday morning quarterback, and suggesting a series of plays that would CYA after the fact is part of the standard issue tool set of politicians. This is evidenced by all the finger pointing at the Bush administration after the initial fighting ceased and occupation began. The question I ponder is: Prior to the vote to authorize the war, how many of those voting asked to see, be briefed on, or review the war strategy; the occupation strategy; and the exit strategy? Starting with the Civil War, we have plenty of historical references to draw upon for examples of outcomes that could have helped in the crafting of an occupation and exit strategy. Did anybody ask these questions prior to the vote, and if they did, who were they and what were the responses of those asked and those answering?

Chapter 4

Campaign Reform

"I've never been able to understand why a Republican contributor is a 'fat cat' and a Democratic contributor of the same amount of money is a 'public-spirited philanthropist.' "

—Ronald Reagan

At a time when I didn't have any gray hair and was an avid reader of United States history, I can remember spending endless summer hours reading from the set of American Heritage color history volumes my mother had purchased for me at the local supermarket. Each week a new volume went on sale, and I couldn't wait to get my hands on it. One of my favorites covered the time period of the Civil War. I loved military history and the politics surrounding that war. I found myself constantly rereading Lincoln's Gettysburg address. Of particular note was a passage Lincoln borrowed from his predecessors that for me will forever ring true as the embodiment of what this great country is all about. "A government of the people, by the people and for the people."

As noble as this statement is, at the birth of our nation it was controversial. Thomas Jefferson, an educated, wealthy landowner, felt that it was irresponsible for the ignorant, common man to be allowed to determine the presidency, whereas John Adams felt that it was the right and duty of all free men to participate in the electoral process, regardless of education, wealth or status (women and slaves excluded). Gradually, over the last 200 years, we as a nation have evolved and the electoral process has been amended to include the voice of all citizens...to an extent!!!

Our Founding Fathers originally envisioned that candidates elected to office would serve one term in office and then return to private life. They never envisioned that public service would end up as a career. Today, we see that public service has morphed into extended terms of office leading to career politicians. This was definitely not what was initially envisioned. Today, we have seen that the longer an elected official remains in office, the more seniority he or she attains and the more power they have. Along with that seniority comes power. That seniority and power are not obtained from or used on behalf of the constituents. More often than not, special interest groups enable the candidate to be reelected via campaign contributions. The voice of the people is no longer the first priority; rather, the desires and interests of major campaign contributors are foremost. In effect, our elected official's votes are compromised at best, legally bribed at worst. The only way to limit this legal bribery is to mandate that any elected official at the federal level must serve a limited time in office. Excluding the presidency, I would suggest that 12 years in office would be appropriate. Any combination of House and Senate positions could be acceptable, as long as time in office is limited to 12 years. Along with this limitation, elected officials should not be allowed to serve on the same committee for more than one term. This would hopefully limit the influence of special interest groups and return the power to the people.

While everyone now has the right to vote, relatively few have the financial ability to sustain a run for elected office. The higher the level of government office sought, the less likely is one's ability to compete. The financial barrier of entry is too prohibitive. True campaign reform was supposed to lessen that barrier.

The Congress, political parties, and presidential candidates for the past decade or more have taken the issue of campaign reform very seriously. They have also found ingenious ways to pay lip service to it while finding covert ways to sidestep real reform. The 527s come to mind. As long as it requires millions upon millions of dollars to launch and sustain a vibrant campaign, true reform will never occur. Thomas Jefferson was ultimately correct in his thinking, regardless of who is allowed to vote — only the wealthy have the wherewithal to run for office.

"The newspaper reported that analysis of Hsu's campaign finance reform records shows he has links to more than $1.8 million in donations to Democrats since 2004.

"He also is credited with raising $850,000 for Clinton's presidential campaign, which announced Monday that it would return all donations linked to Hsu."

"The newspaper reports that a company run by Norman Hsu, who donated nearly $2 million to Democratic candidates since 2004 — including presidential hopeful Sen. Hillary Clinton — recently received $40 million from a Madison Avenue investment fund run by Joel Rosenman, one of the creators of the fabled Woodstock rock festival in 1969."

The previous few passages were reported by CNN website in 2008. As for Hillary, I believe she once said lobbyist's donations were valid, because lobbyists represent people too! My guess is that if you were to list every politician and their respective campaign contributors and their voting record on every piece of legislation, you could probably easily find a direct correlation between the way they voted and their source of campaign funds. The constituents be damned. This theory probably does not apply to all of our elected officials, but I would bet that it applies to most, at all levels of government.

The 2008 presidential campaign kicked off before the 2004 Presidential election outcome was even determined. Everyone in the world, despite Hillary's denials, knew she was running for President in '08. Before her first elected term as U.S. senator from New York, she declared that she would fill out her term in office. Before her second elected term, she modified that declaration saying that she couldn't promise filling out her term if elected. I'll say it again for emphasis. I felt cheated by Hillary, because she spent far too much time, energy, and focus on her own national ambition everywhere outside New York State. She did this on our dime. I would have had more respect for her if she had resigned her position as an elected official before engaging in her run for president. If it appears that I am picking on Hillary, well, I guess I am, but only because she made it so evident and appeared to have no remorse. Just for the record, I am against every candidate who holds an elected office while running for reelection or election to another position. They simply cannot focus on their primary responsibility to represent the populace who elected them if they are being distracted by a campaign. There should be a way to accomplish campaigning while doing the nation's business without distraction.

We hear it every campaign as the media covers the potential presidential candidates: so and so has accumulated an additional $25 million in their campaign fund this quarter, and so and so will probably be forced to drop out of the running because his war chest is so far behind everyone else's. To what end does all this funding and campaigning serve? You might argue that this existing process gives the public the opportunity to become familiar with the candidates and is the start of a vetting process to eventually whittle down the numbers to a select two. I will argue that it is a self-destructive process that only rewards those with the deepest pockets, not necessarily the best ideas. Too many people with good ideas and real platforms are automatically locked out of the process, especially the average citizen who doesn't stand a chance because he does not have access to Fort Knox. I am of the opinion that in order for the average Joe to have a chance to run effectively for public office, there needs to be a standard set of game rules in place to ensure that all who choose to run have a somewhat level playing field. I say somewhat, because fame and notoriety will always exist for some, but ideas, morality, character, and a work ethic are available to all on an equal basis. I believe that the ability to be heard and to get the message out is the limiting factor of the average Joe. This is the greatest "barrier of entry"— cost considerations. I'll throw out some ideas that should generate debate, perhaps even lead to campaign reform that will benefit the entire country.

Let's start at the local level. To even be considered for a run for local office, or any office for that matter, I think it is only appropriate and fair that a potential candidate put forth a clear platform. First of all, a full disclosure of financials, a detailed resume of employment history, education and associations/affiliations, along with a qualifying summarization explaining why he or she is seeking public office should be publicly posted on a website. In addition to the above, a detailed "candidate's platform" should be posted. This platform would serve to communicate the candidate's stand on issues, resolutions, goals, and objectives of his or her campaign for office. Once these are posted, the only modifications allowed should require a notated reference of date and time of modification. There can only be additions to this document, and deletions of any sort should not be allowed. Once a candidate states a position it will always be there for posterity and reference. A change in position would require the candidate to explain why this became necessary. Let's call this "truth in advertising."

At all levels of public office seeking, matching public funds from a pool (public campaign offset fund) could be obtained by a candidate if appropriate levels of petitioned signatures and campaign donations are achieved by a specified deadline. Campaign spending could be set to a certain limit, specific to the size of the geographic area for which the sought public office serves. As a public service, provided by the media specific to these geographic areas, a series of televised debates could be aired up until the election. Campaign contributions could be limited to amounts no greater than $5 per social security number, collected and disbursed by a non-partisan organization. Media advertising such as radio and television could be made available to all qualified candidates with roughly the equivalent time slots on the same media in equal amounts at a discounted rate. It would be up to the candidate to determine how to maximize his media advertising dollar spend. All aired media purchases could be made only through the nonpartisan organization disbursement process. All nondisbursed funds would be returned to the public campaign offset fund for reinvestment and future use by anyone in future campaigns. There should be no lobbyist, PAC, or interest group contributions allowed. Period!

To address my pet peeve of candidates who already hold elected office while campaigning for reelection or another office, the following could be put in place. A campaign season limited in duration to one year could be mandated by legislation. Since all candidates MUST post their platforms on the internet and via other media, this can be the first step in the campaign season. All primaries should be restructured to be held within the same week, six months before Election Day. By doing this, every participant in the campaign process will be afforded the same opportunities for exposure under the same financial constraints. Let credentials, platform, and message, rather than deep financial pockets determine the outcome.

I know that this idea is utopian and idealistic at best; however, the spirit of such an idea should be implemented. Any attempts to advertise or campaign via 527s, organizations such as Swift Boat Veterans, Move-on.org, or any special-interest group, regardless of candidate affiliation or declared nonaffiliation, could be allowed provided they all carry a full-screen, ten-second disclaimer as such: "The following is a paid political advertisement paid for by xxxxxxx. This advertisement is neither sanctioned nor approved by any candidate. The content is generated by xxxxxxx and may in fact be nonverifiable, biased, and unsupported. Viewer discretion is advised."

Additionally, any spot that runs should be subject to a donation to the public campaign offset fund equivalent to ten times the cost of the advertisement, as well as a donation in the same amount to the U.S. Treasury earmarked for use by Social Security. For example, if a 30-second ad on TV cost $10,000, then $100,000 would be donated to the public campaign offset fund and $100,000 would be donated to the U.S. Treasury. The media running the advertisement would be responsible to ensure that the donations have been received before running the ad, or else they (the media) would also be subject to a fine (non-tax-deductible donation) equivalent to twice the original donation amount. A minimum donation amount, say $50,000, could be established in order to inhibit abuse of the process.

The whole purpose of these guidelines is to level the playing field for all who want to participate in the democratic process, and not limit the process to the millionaires club. Let us not forget this is a government OF the people, BY the people and FOR the people, so PEOPLE get involved and let's govern!

Chapter 5

Federal Deficit

"It is incumbent on every generation to pay its own debts as it goes. A principle which if acted on would save one-half the wars of the world."

—Thomas Jefferson

L et's talk a little bit about the federal deficit. Do you own a credit card? Most likely you do, and as most households in the United States have credit cards, so does the federal government. The only difference between the federal government's credit card and yours is that the government's card isn't issued by MasterCard, Visa, or American Express. The government's card is issued by you and used by your elected officials. Typically, the president, on an annual basis, develops a budget that dictates the amount of money he wants to spend to provide for the services that you the citizens require or want the government to provide. The theory (not to be confused with reality) is that all services will be paid for through the collection of taxes. When theory is reality, the amount of taxes collected covers the cost of the expenses provided for by the budget. This would be called a balanced budget. In some cases, rare as it may seem, the government actually collects more in tax revenues than it spends. This results in a budget surplus, a good thing.

In really good economic times, usually when the stock market is performing well, people make more money, both through investments and wages. Taxes collected on wages and investments contribute to increased amounts of tax revenues. People also spend more, generating greater amounts of sales taxes. When stocks that you own appreciate in value and you sell them for a profit, the government collects a capital gains tax. When stocks pay a dividend, that is also taxed by the government. When you invest in business by purchasing stocks, the companies use that money to grow their businesses, purchasing equipment and hiring more employees. This generates more tax revenues for the government. It is called the multiplier effect, and the economy grows. Unfortunately, much as politicians would like you to believe, the government, and more so the president, has little control over how the economy performs. The president is usually relegated to happy benefactor of a vibrant economy, or unhappy victim of a poorly performing economy. Political parties love to attribute a good economy to a President when their party controls the presidency, and blame the president and the party who happens to be seated during a poor economy. This is not entirely fair. The Federal Reserve and the Treasury have more of an influence over the economy, but they are supposed to be a neutral influence as far as political parties are concerned. Congress, on the other hand, has the most influence over the economy via legislation and budget. Legislation can drive the budget via tax policy and spending (budget appropriations).

When we spend more than we take in, it is known as a deficit, usually not a good thing. Let's continue with the budget process. The budget developed by the President is submitted to Congress for approval and must be approved before it can become law. This is where the fun starts. Your elected officials, who must approve the budget, contrive to make the budget a better bill for a number of reasons. Two of the most important are political ideology and pork (see an explanation in Social Security, Chapter 11). This process requires horse-trading between political parties (political ideology) before the budget is deemed acceptable for approval. The result is usually a flagrant disregard for the taxpayer's contribution and an increase in deficit spending. It is the same as if you charged in a month more than you can pay off at the time the charge bill arrives. Sad to say, too many American households send the minimum required payment and pay an exorbitant amount of finance charges on the unpaid balance. This is also called deficit spending.

Since the federal government cannot legally spend what it doesn't have, it must borrow the additional funds needed to cover debt. It does this by selling United States backed securities, payable at a future point in time at various interest rates. I'm sure you are all familiar with U.S. savings bonds. We usually associate these with gifts to someone for some special occasion. They are typically in the amount of $50 to $500. The federal government, in order to finance deficit, sells Treasury bills/bonds typically in denominations of thousands of dollars. Well, the attraction for someone (not usually an individual, but rather a country) to purchase our T-bills (debt) is purely the faith in the national stability of both our government and our economy.

This is good news and bad. Good in the sense that other countries are willing to finance our reckless spending habits, bad, in that eventually we have to pay off our obligations to these purchasers of our debt. Where do you think that comes from? Why it comes from you the taxpayers in the form of higher taxes and reduced services, at least when it comes time to pay the piper. Every time we increase the deficit amount, our dollar becomes worth a little less compared to the currencies of other countries whose spending habits do not generate deficits. This is a simplified explanation of the United States currency valuation; a detailed explanation would require an economics text. Right now, China and other countries own so much of our debt that they may no longer want to continue to willingly purchase more. If they stop purchasing our debt, the piper will have to make a house call sooner rather than later.

One of my biggest pet peeves about the way our electoral process functions is how it contributes to budget spending. It is both a cause and an effect of our electoral process. In order for the ordinary citizen to run for office he must have built a sizable campaign war chest. We have all seen the recent figures that presidential candidates compiled nine months before the primaries; a few candidates already amassed $25+ million in campaign war chests. As for those potential candidates with less than $10 million .... forget it. Are we, as a country, out of our collective minds? Even the costs for running a campaign at local levels have recently exceeded astronomical amounts, millions of dollars! How the hell can the ordinary citizen even begin to think about running for public office?

The point is, to be elected campaign contributions must reach a stratospheric level. When the stakes become that high, it stands to reason that our noble elected officials (not all, mind you) have accepted contributions from sources with some special interests. While it is understood that this in no way obligates an elected official to do the bidding of such interests, it is also understood that they know where their bread is buttered. If you check out special interest contributions to candidates, you will most likely find that they hedge their bets by donating to many candidates of all party affiliations, so as not to appear unfair. Let's face it; this is nothing more than legalized bribery. At some point, at some time, the favor is most likely returned, and when it is, it most likely costs the taxpayer both in monies spent, and in inefficiencies.

To keep the loyal constituents who were responsible for putting their candidate in office happy, the elected official will fight long and hard to place some tag line (they are now called earmarks) in the budget to allocate x number of dollars for his local district. This is in addition to the earmarks for lobbyists. In many cases, I suspect that you find out about this the same way that I do. Before reelections I am inundated by my locally elected officials with newsletters proclaiming all the good they have accomplished during their current term, and the amount of dollars they have bravely fought for to enhance the values or standard of living in my area. They have brought home the bacon in the form of pork barrel spending, and believe me, it isn't free. You are paying for it via deficit spending. It would be extremely interesting to see how many of these allocations would pass if they had to stand on their own merit, instead of being included as a precondition for passage of necessary, functional, and rational legislation.

If the president had line-item veto power, we might have tax surpluses instead of deficits. Maybe we as taxpayers should demand that our elected officials become less frivolous with our hard-earned tax money by passing legislation something like the following: If in the course of budget resolution, the Congress finds it necessary to approve and/or submit legislation authorizing a budget that requires funding over and above the projected revenues for the time period covering expenditures (deficit spending), then Congress shall be authorized to issue interest bearing bonds via the U.S. Treasury Department with a return no greater than 1 % to acquire the necessary deficit funding. If the funds are not acquired within a one-month time period from issuance of such offering, then the issue will immediately sunset and the President will be required to submit a balanced budget within one month's time, which cannot be overridden by Congress.

Let's put it simply, any expenditure should be able to stand on its own merit. I firmly believe that every budget line item should be voted on individually. Some necessary appropriations may at times seem to make no sense to different groups of people. I understand that there are regional differences between a farmer in the Midwest and a socialite on the Upper East Side of New York City. The farmer might consider New York City transit issues overblown, since he may never have ridden a subway, or even care to. The NYC socialite wouldn't have a clue what a cow manure driven fuel cell is, and maybe not even what a cow is for that matter. I think you get the point that compromise and comprehension are necessary to support a wide variety of valid fundamental programs and expenditures that benefit the populace as a whole.

Being fiscally responsible might result in the ability of the government to spend our money on programs, such as Social Security and Medicare (absolute necessities) that are more important to our future and the future of generations to come.

Our elected officials must be fiscally responsible. Balanced budgets are a necessity. We cannot continually spend away the future of our children. We must put an end to earmarks. There will of course be times when deficit spending becomes necessary to fund programs critical to our nation's well-being. These deficits should become part of the next budget and the revenue for covering these deficit expenditures must be identified. To prevent unnecessary expenditures and assure the population that their money is being well spent, every expense item in all bills passed by Congress must be published for all to see before passage. If they (our elected representatives) cannot be fiscally responsible on their own, then maybe it will be necessary to float a national referendum to decide upon the implementation of the line item veto. This may not be the solution either, as we may have elected a fiscally irresponsible president (I can name a recent few) who will also not abide by our wishes. In a case as this, the only solution is to vote the bums out of office.

Recently, we have been faced with economic volatility stemming what is called a "subprime mortgage." The phenomena is the result of a euphoric economic boom time not only in this country, but worldwide. As we all know, the value of homes dramatically increased year over year, allowing any and every homeowner to view this asset as a new-found piggy bank via home equity loans. The demand for homes seemed like it would never end, and everyone who had any money for a down payment, along with those without a pot to piss in (also expressed as NINJA loans — no income, no job, no assets) would easily qualify for a mortgage, no questions asked. Builders and mortgage lenders were so eager to sell their product (and pocket easy profits and commissions) that a loan could be fabricated for anyone, as long as he was breathing. Irresponsible practices resulting in unscrupulous lending resulted in (to borrow a well-used term) "irrational exuberance."

Prospective home buyers took out loans with ridiculously low teaser variable rates, intending to refinance at an affordable fixed rate before the variable rates reset at an astronomically high rate. Anyone with half a brain would know they couldn't afford these loans. This whole premise was based upon an ever-increasing home value. After a year or two, the expectation was that the home would appreciate so much that equity would have built up and refinancing at a lower rate would be a snap. Unfortunately for everyone the house of cards collapsed when the demand for housing dried up, relative to supply. Prices began to fall as opposed to appreciating, and the underlying pyramid of leveraged financial vehicles no longer held value as borrowers defaulted on their loans and foreclosures ensued. People with variable interest rate mortgages whose mortgages reset to exorbitant levels could no longer refinance or service their debt. They were upside down so to speak.

People who used their home's established equity as personal piggy banks, while maybe not in financial trouble, also found themselves upside down as home values dropped. This resulted in the inability to sell their homes without taking a loss, or being forced to hold on to their homes but servicing a large loan that they couldn't afford. This certainly put a crimp on disposable income and led to a downturn in the economy as people cut back on spending. Consumer spending, by the way, accounts for approximately 70% of the U.S. economy. There is really a lot more to this story, but for the sake of keeping it simple I left out most of the technical details.

In the end (which hasn't fully occurred yet), the taxpayer via the Federal Reserve, the U.S. Treasury, and a weakened dollar will pay for the sins of others' greed, the failure of federal agencies to exercise their responsibilities, irresponsibly enacted legislation, ignorant politicians, outright fraud, and stupidity. This will also end up increasing the federal deficit. The hoopla that this whole experience caused will eventually result in additional Federal regulation of the mortgage industry via the Federal Housing Agency, the Securities and Exchange Commission, and/or a host of existing or new agencies.

I suggest that there may be a silver lining in this dark cloud! Albeit a costly exercise, we may with a little restructuring of federal policy turn this money-losing situation into a strong wealth-building program to benefit both the consumer and social programs such as Medicare. We have already seen the poor result of mortgage lenders and commercial banks when left to their own self-regulatory policies (in my mind, this is still a debatable point, as federal government agencies in the name of "social engineering" may well be responsible for much of this mess). Let's take matters into our own hands and let the federal government (I can't believe that I am actually saying this) get into the game of mortgage lending via the FHA and other quasi-government agencies, some of which already exist. For private low cost (affordable) mortgages, the quasi-federal agencies like Fannie Mae and Freddie Mac (which we have already bailed out) could issue low cost mortgages under stringent guidelines. A caveat to accepting a loan of this sort would be for the homeowner to not only pay off the loan, but also be required to forego a percentage of profit, or agree to pay a fixed percent of the proceeds from a sale, to the government. The government could optionally either sell these securities on the open market for a profit or continue to service these loans until they are retired. A percentage of any profit could be directed to fund social programs, offsetting tax increases necessary to fund these programs.

Over the last year, our financial system has been in meltdown mode. We have witnessed the collapse of IndyMac Bank, Bear Sterns, Lehman Brothers, Fannie Mae, Freddie Mac, and AIG. All of this stems from the subprime mortgage disaster. Thanks to the work of Federal Reserve Chairman Ben Bernanke and Secretary of the Treasury Henry Paulson, a complete global financial meltdown has been averted, at least temporarily. The federal government took over IndyMac Bank, bailed out Fannie Mae, Freddie Mac, and AIG, and arranged a subsidized bailout of Bear Sterns. Lehman Brothers was allowed to file for bankruptcy. There was a lot of controversy as to how it was determined which company to save and which to let fail. Bernanke and Paulson acted in the overall interest of not only the United States, but also the rest of the world's financial community. They did act quickly and decisively, and were not burdened by partisan politics. They were questioned and second-guessed about their decisions. Congress's nose is out of joint because they were not consulted prior to these decisions. Harry Reid, Senate majority leader, in reference to the magnitude and complexity of the crisis stated, "We don't know what to do." So much for leadership! Maybe that explains why Bernanke and Paulson acted solo.

I am against big government, but if programs can be self-sufficient or generate a profit for the citizens, then I believe they are at least worthy of a look. What we need is a government that works for the people, not a government that mortgages our future with unserviceable deficits.

Last year, both Paulson and Bernanke were grilled by a host of elected officials at a hearing of the Banking Committee chaired by Congressman Barney Frank. This unfortunately is where politics rears its ugly head. After listening to the hearing for over two hours, I came away disgusted. Every politician lived up to his calling. They were each given five minutes to comment and ask questions of Paulson and Bernanke regarding their proposed bailout plan. They all either thanked Paulson and Bernanke for their efforts or criticized their efforts for a variety of reasons. Most grandstanded, making sure that they were on record with their self-devised miracle solutions, lobbying efforts for women- and minority-owned business, blaming Republicans, Democrats, Wall Street, and anyone they could think of, but absolving themselves of any blame. They all voiced skepticism of the plan and begged for assurances that it would work. A few actually exhibited extensive knowledge and comprehension of just how serious an issue this was for the country. It was a supreme waste of Paulson and Bernanke's valuable time, and I heartily felt sorry for them. Our two presidential candidates contributed nothing meaningful or constructive to the debate, probably because they are both clueless when it comes to the economy and Wall Street. The only thing that they know about Wall Street and the financial industry is that they are a source of big campaign donations. Our esteemed President will address the nation tonight. If his speech isn't written by Bernanke and Paulson, then that will prove to be a waste of time also.

What Bernanke and Paulson tried to convey to everyone without causing a panic is that the "Plan" needs to be approved post haste, and is not a sure thing, but rather the best option at this time under these particular circumstances. What they politely refrained from telling everyone was that if you don't sign on to this real fast, the credit market, which is currently barely functioning now, will cease to function all together. It will be only a matter of time before small businesses start to lay off workers, and fail to meet payroll, accounts payable, and debt service. They will hoard their capital, close their doors, and fail at an unprecedented rate. We will no longer be looking at a recession, but rather a global depression greater in magnitude and length than anything we could imagine. (These are some of the same conditions that can lead to regional and global conflict. Unfortunately, war is usually a great way to kick-start a sagging economy. War redirects attention and resources and provides for employment opportunities of all varieties. It is a far less desirable substitute for free-market capitalism, but it does put people back to work.)

This, or maybe something equally as drastic, may be what they would have liked to say, but didn't so as not to start a panic. They realized that many of the safeguards, rules, and restrictions that everyone wants in the legislation have not been defined but need to be put in place. They also realize that that is best left to the politicians, because it will take many weeks, if not months, to hash out. Paulson and Bernanke realize that they don't have weeks, they have days. For all their grandstanding, the politicians will vote relatively soon, and they will vote yes to a $700 billion expenditure, because they in the words of Harry Reid, Senate majority leader, "We don't know what to do."

As the average American taxpayer, I am outraged at the prospect of having to bail out the irresponsible mortgage lenders, federal agencies who were asleep at the switch, Fannie and Freddie, Barney Frank (who assured us that we were in no danger of insolvency), Wall Street banks and brokerage firms, and lastly, the irresponsible home buyers who were way in over their heads. Like all of you who have been financially responsible and lived within your means, we are the people being dumped on. Our homes have lost significant value, our retirement accounts have shrunk drastically, and we are saddled with a debt burden like we have never seen before. Even if the bailout plan ends up costing the taxpayer nothing, it will take many years before our financial health even begins to return to where it was — unfortunately for too many of us, pushing our retirement age back many more years.

Our elected officials and perspective candidates must be held accountable for their spending plans. We must demand detailed budget plans from all candidates and elected officials. We can no longer afford to continuously run budget deficits and expect to prosper let alone survive as a nation. Campaign promises are usually long on rhetoric and short on substance. We have to challenge our candidates in order to prevent ourselves and our future from being shortchanged

One last thought that I need to express here. While it does not necessarily fall under the topic of federal deficit, it could affect the federal budget and hence the deficit in the long run. At the current time, the banks have the opportunity to borrow short term from the Fed discount window at a rate of 2% (now down to 0 -.25 %). If I were to go to the bank to take out a loan or mortgage, the bank would charge me around 5% or 6 % interest. What I find incredible is that the banks borrow from the Fed (our money), and turn around and lend (our money) to us at 3% to 5% higher than they borrowed it for. In essence, we are paying a third party (the bank), to borrow our own money. These are the same institutions that so deftly lost billions on their lending practices and currently require another $700 billion of our money to rescue them.

Our housing market is in the toilet, and so is our economy because of it (thanks to the banks, mortgage brokers, and highly irresponsible social policy that advocated giving loans to those who could in no way afford them). How about, if instead of having to get a mortgage from the bank, people could go directly to a federal agency to apply for a mortgage? Provided the federal agency followed stringent approval guidelines (no NINJA type loans, 20% down) and applicants were fully qualified, loans could be approved for first-time buyers, or for that matter all buyers at the Fed discount window rate. The loans, not only for first-time home buyers of residential property, could be given on condition that when a property is sold, the borrower might be required to repay the government an additional .5% to 1% of any realized gain, in return for receiving this low cost loan.

This type of policy would do a number of positive things. It would allow all buyers to secure affordable financing and would spur the housing market (including job creation). It would give more people an opportunity to participate responsibly in the American Dream, and it would provide a source of income from the premium derived from the sale of these properties. This would help to self-fund the program. This is a perk for American citizens. After all, it is our money in the first place, and why should the banks (who have demonstrated their irresponsibility) be allowed to double dip at our expense? The banks could provide funding and make their profits in the mortgage market for any mortgages other than those given by the federal agency.

As of early 2009, the Congress has seemed to come to an agreement to pass legislation allowing for a $780 billion stimulus package which would supposedly stimulate the economy, provide approximately 4–4.5 million new jobs, cut taxes, extend unemployment benefits, give healthcare to those who cannot afford it, fund infrastructure projects, and provide green jobs. The Republicans have been framed as the roadblock to this legislation, because they objected to the spending provisions in this bill. They have proclaimed that this bill represents a spending package that encompasses all the programs that the Democrats could not pass through Congress on their own merit. Obama has put enormous pressure on both sides to pass this legislation in order to stave off a disaster that will negatively impact the country's economic status for years to come. I am tremendously disheartened that he has resorted to this type of scare tactic to force through what I consider to be irresponsible legislation. In this instance, the Republicans are more than right in their objections. The measures in this bill are not stimulus related, but pure unadulterated, reckless spending on a very grand scale. Yesterday, Obama himself told the Democratic caucus that this stimulus package was a spending package. Apparently he did not see anything wrong with saddling the taxpayers (our children and grand-children) with this future debt that will not appropriately address the true needs of this legislation.

The Republicans held out against the will of Nancy Pelosi and Harry Reid, and a compromise (lower and more focused spending via tax cuts and stimulus) has been reached. I have yet to see the entire bill, but I can only bet that it is still loaded to the gills with pork. Am I cynical? You bet I am. Am I upset and disgusted? You bet I am. The public, in a poll released recently (that I saw on the CNN website), was 51% to 34% in favor of a stimulus package. When informed of just a few of the items in the package, that approval rating slipped to 34%. This was a Demo-crat-generated bill that was preloaded with nonsensical spending and is disingenuous. The taxpayer deserves better, but with the Democrats writing legislation of this sort and in control of both houses of Congress, I fear that we, the taxpayer, will for at least the next four years get the short end of the stick. Once again, there is a demonstrated need for statesmen as opposed to the politicians that we are stuck with.

Chapter 6

It's the Global Economy, Stupid!

"Build a better mousetrap, and the world will beat a path to your door."

—Ralph Waldo Emerson

One of the most important ills that have beset our great country is the loss of manufacturing jobs. I can remember when Pittsburg, Ohio, and Indiana meant heavy industry; steel mills were all over the landscape. Detroit meant autos, and lots of them. Texas and Oklahoma meant oil and gas. New Jersey meant oil refineries and chemical factories as far as the eye could see along the New Jersey Turnpike. There were shipyards in New York, New Jersey, Virginia, Louisiana, Texas, California, and Maine, to name a few places. All were beehives of heavy industry. Few remain today.

I can remember there used to be something called the U.S. Merchant Marine, U.S. flagged ships crewed by U.S. merchant seamen. Everything was always under construction: the Eisenhower Interstate System, buildings, parks, infrastructure, etc. Names like Caterpillar, Michigan, Bucyrus-Erie, to name a few, were commonplace on heavy-duty construction equipment. All meant good paying jobs and trickle-down supplier employment. Unfortunately, I can also remember all too frequently the unions of these workers calling for strikes over wages and benefits. Some names remain, but now most of these companies, their products, and their jobs are gone, replaced by foreign names such as Toyota, Hyundai, Honda, Tohatsu, and Kubota. Steel comes from

Japan and South America; ships are built in Asia and crewed by non-U.S. seamen. Some oil still comes from Texas and Alaska, but most comes from South America, the Middle East, Africa, and soon Russia. The centers of heavy industry along our coasts, waterways, and harbors are now replaced by Rust Belts, condos, and ocean walks. Centers of former heavy industry in Ohio and Michigan are now ghost towns, with few to no prospects of revival.

The world has changed significantly over the last 50 years. We have gone from an analog society of snail mail to a digital society of text messaging. We are a world that has come to expect instant gratification with the click of a mouse, a swipe of a credit card, cellular phones, text messaging, video iPods, and internet iPhones. Ozzie and Harriet make way for the Jetsons! This all comes at a price. That price is both by necessity one that we can afford, and one that we cannot afford, at least without making appropriate adjustments and accommodations. How did we come so far so fast? Technological advancements, that's how.

Rapid advancements in technology have resulted in equally rapid gains in productivity, enabling reductions in cost and affordable prices for high-tech manufactured goods. Sometime in the future, probably sooner rather than later, iPhone-type devices will become so inexpensive that they will become standard equipment for everybody, much in the same way that everyone carries a cell phone now. This is great, you say. I agree. But, where are these devices manufactured? More than likely, they will be manufactured in China, Vietnam, Thailand, or some other country. Most probably the only work done by Americans, other than in-store sales personnel, is the product and packaging design work done by skilled high-tech labor. The reason that the product will be affordable is because the manufacturing process is outsourced to a factory in a foreign country where labor is cheap.

In the new world of the global economy, this is the new paradigm.

Gone are the days when design, engineering and manufacturing were all done by American workers. For companies to be competitive on price (and survive in the marketplace), price point is the dominant factor and labor cost is the primary cost variable. The relative costs associated with the use of American labor have put us at a distinct competitive disadvantage with the rest of the world. The United States workforce must make the appropriate adjustments and accommodations to become competitive and survive. Gone forever are the days of a massive nonskilled or semiskilled labor force based upon manufacturing. The typical blue-collar unionized labor force of 50 years ago simply cannot compete with the workforce of today's global economy. This is not to say that all is lost for American labor, but we need to do some real soul searching and make the hard adjustments necessary to enable competitive American labor employment. We need to do this quickly, otherwise we will all be flipping burgers at the local fast food establishment.

I have possible remedies for our economic survival. The first step in going forward in this process is more psychological than physical. It is also probably the hardest to accept.

I have stated it already, but will repeat it with emphasis. The typical blue-collar unionized labor force of 50 years ago simply cannot compete in the workforce of today's global economy. Your father's Oldsmobile no longer exists, and neither do the assembly line jobs that produced it. Furthermore, those jobs are most likely gone forever. You would have to be delusional to believe any political candidate who espouses the belief that these lost jobs will be restored at the same income levels that existed when they were lost. Until unions come to their senses and decide to live in the here and now by cutting wage and benefit demands to a competitive level commensurate to the skill level appropriate for the job, more jobs will continue to be lost. As a matter of fact, in the last few years, two-thirds of the unionized autoworker jobs have been eliminated. The Germans bought Chrysler and after a couple of years couldn't wait to unload it due to associated organized labor costs. It still remains to be seen whether Chrysler can continue to be a viable entity, but I suspect it will be dismantled and sold off in pieces to foreign companies, resulting in even more job losses.

The following is a very brief recap of history for the purpose of illustrating my train of thought. Prior to and at the beginning of the industrial revolution of this country, the populace was employed primarily in agriculture. With the advances in technology such as steam power and mechanical devices that made automation and economies of scale possible; factories sprang up like weeds in the cities. The need to employ massive amounts of people was filled from a pool of immigrants and farmers. The factories at the time were sweatshops with little to absolutely no regard for the safety, health, or welfare of their employees. Working conditions were generally deplorable, child labor was rampant, terrible accidents resulting in death and dismemberment were common, pay was minuscule, benefits were nonexistent and retirement was usually due to death or ill health. For the most part, the only persons to truly benefit from the fruits of labor were the factory owners. Government, both at the state and federal levels, had little incentive to meddle in commerce and provide any sort of safeguards for those employed by the factory owners, as the owners were usually strong supporters of the politicians (lobbying was already in effect way back then). Most of the jobs in the factories were of the unskilled labor sort, and if a worker was not producing fast enough, he/she could easily be replaced from an ever-expanding pool of job seekers.

The economics of labor supply and demand benefited the owners, leaving the workers with little incentive to protest conditions. These conditions prevailed until skilled workers with a trade, such as shoemakers, banded together to demand better wages and working conditions. Trade unions began to take hold and strikes became a threat to owners. Organized labor was born, along with collective bargaining. Eventually, legislation to provide labor safeguards was introduced and passed. Labor unions played a vital role in vastly improving the rights, safety, and benefit of the working man. From the 1860s through the 1950s, organized labor grew in leaps and bounds. Union members grew in numbers, and union leaders became equivalent to heads of state. What ensued over the course of a century was a 180-degree reversal of power between worker and owner.

It proved to be a false positive for unions. When the United States became the arsenal of democracy, factories shifted production from consumer goods to military wares. As American men left their jobs to enter military service, women replaced men on the factory floor. At war's end, the men gradually replaced the women on the factory floor, life returned to normal, and the baby boom ensued. Unions were in their hey-day, as demand for consumer goods flourished. Factories were running at full speed to meet demand, employment was full, and under threat of strike, business bowed to the demands of labor's ever-increasing demands for wages and benefits. Good times were had by all ... for a while.

Union leadership lost its focus on the primary reason for its existence, the welfare of its membership. Leadership became too powerful. Instead of negotiating reasonably to ensure survival of itself and the corporations it bargained with, unions became greedy and dictatorial, eventually poisoning the goose that laid the golden eggs. Just look at union membership numbers from post World War II to the present. The decline is telling.

It was about this time that two things happened that would forever change the course of world economics. The baby boomers were growing up and the Marshall Plan began to take roots. For the most part, the ravages of war destroyed the economies of Europe and Asia. Having seen what happened as a result of World War I, where Germany was saddled by its victors with unrealistic war reparations and an inability to repay or service those demands, leading ultimately to World War II, the United States was determined to rebuild the economies and sovereignty of defeated former foes. While United States factories were considered the cream of the crop, they were also aging and in need of technological upgrade. Capital reinvestment requirements from retained earnings competed with wage and benefits demands of labor. All too often, labor won out. Meanwhile, the infrastructure rebuilds of our former foes yielded state of the art factories that churned out goods looking for a market. Guess where that market was?

Before and immediately post World War II, imports from Europe consisted mainly of luxury automobiles such as Rolls-Royce, Mercedes, BMW, Volvo, SAAB, and some Italian models. Auto imports from Japan were virtually nonexistent. As far as Americans were concerned, Detroit was the automotive capital of the world. What we did start to see from Japan, however, were massive amounts of inexpensive, cheap, junk trinket type products. Collectively, these were of little to no concern to Americans, and as far as a market threat goes, these products and their country of origin were under the radar screen.

What we should have realized was that the pre–World War II barriers to trade, such as protective tariffs and distance, which pretty much kept us insulated from serious competition, were being breached. Not only were the Japanese eager to implement our production models, but they were extremely eager students as well. Remember all the photos and news stories about the Japanese businessmen coming over here to tour our factories? They always came over loaded with cameras. The cameras returned home full of examples of our automated production lines. Those photos were soon to become reality with a big emphasis placed upon quality and miniaturization.

The initial products that the Japanese produced were not exactly new, in concept or technology, just more compact and attractive. The Japanese culture also lent itself to a very cost-effective workforce, which asked, "What can I do for the company?" and not, "What is the least I can do and be compensated the most for?" What the Japanese did to us was a replicate of what we did to the British after we gained our independence. The Japanese began to produce in volume products that were of little consequence and competition to our overall industrial base and markets. The cheap quality and cost-wise trinkets were well-received by our consumer base and recognized exactly for what they were.

The important takeaway here was that the Japanese gained a foothold into our markets, one that became bigger and more competitive each succeeding year. The Japanese understood just how to satisfy our consumer wants with products tailored to our consumer household budgets. This is where the baby boomers and history came into play.

Back in the early 1970s, a number of factors began to shape the future of our economy and industrial base.

Factor one was:

Gasoline was retailing for about 25¢ a gallon. There were even price wars where if you filled up your tank, you received a free quart bottle of Coke®, or a free drinking glass. These times I remember well. "Muscle" cars rolled off the Detroit assembly line. These cars were equipped with V8 engines, were fast, and were the envy of the world.

Factor two was:

Baby boomers were growing up and turning into a tremendous consumer base with needs all their own. They were also becoming better educated then their parents. Where many parents achieved a high school education, their dreams for their children aimed higher. They wanted a college education for their offspring. While this was admirable, it was also expensive. Up until this time, families typically owned a family car. Baby boomer families typically had multiple children clustered within a few years of each other. Family budgets became strained as the need to support everyone's needs from a single paycheck became tougher and tougher. As the children reached the age where driving became a necessity in order to attend college, go to part-time jobs, and socialize, the demands for the family car became unsupportable with a single vehicle. The family paycheck could not support the demands for multiple expensive American vehicles either. An alternative to an American car was a less expensive Japanese import. Sure, everyone knew that these alternatives were of lesser quality, but they typically came equipped with a standard AM/FM radio, often times with a cassette deck as well. American car dealers demanded a premium for such extras. The Japanese imports were mostly less expensive than their American counterparts and got far better gas mileage. They were an affordable alternative for the tight household budget.

History also played a part in driving demand for imports. When the Iranians took over our embassy in Teheran and the oil embargo ensued, the demand for cars with better gas mileage gave the import dealers a ready-made market. As gas lines grew and became the norm, so did the sales lines at Datsun, Toyota, and Honda. American manufacturers caught totally off guard responded with diesel engines and a rush to design compact and more fuel-efficient vehicles. What resulted was less than satisfactory to the American consumer. The Japanese were light years ahead of us. Our answer was the Vega, Maverick, Gremlin, and Pinto, all of which were poor competition to the Japanese. Meanwhile the Japanese responded with better quality, durability, style, gas mileage, standard equipment, and increased market share.

This was America's first real taste of foreign competition in a yet unrecognized global economy. The Americans lost on two fronts but gained on one in this dynamic. We lost jobs and market share, but gained in standard of living as the Japanese imported cars provided the American consumer with an alternative utility at an affordable price. The competitive advantage the Japanese had was not due solely to workforce productivity or labor cost.

The steel that was used for the cars was also a major contributing factor to the cost advantage. The Japanese automakers were not importing steel from the United States; rather, they were using domestically produced product. After, the Japanese steel mills were built with the most modern technology available at the time. Their mills were far more efficient than those of America's. The combination of technological innovation and implementation along with a less expensive workforce would result in increasing American job losses. We as a country have seen our factories close, assembly lines shut down, and industries disappear. As the once sleepy Asian and Pacific Rim countries watched the Japanese model of success take hold, they too have awakened to become the Asian tigers replicating Japan's model for success.

Today, the American consumer satisfies his/her appetite for products produced by these countries in an ever-increasing amount. As we import more products, we export more assembly line jobs and dollars. The high-paying skilled and semiskilled assembly line jobs have been replaced by an ever-increasing low wage/low skill service industry and an ever-increasing trade deficit. Our lifeblood and technological prowess are being sucked right out of us. You may be tempted to blame our NAFTA and free trade agreements for this, but I caution against such logic. Our standard of living has improved tremendously due to the lower cost, higher quality products we import. By railing against NAFTA et al, we simply hide behind our ignorance, move closer to isolationism/protectionism, and fail to address what got us here in the first place.

We instead need to identify what must be done to preserve our economic engine, competitive advantage, standard of living, and dominance as the world's economic powerhouse. Beware of politicians who promise you that jobs will be restored or that it is through no fault of your own that your jobs have unfairly been exported out of the country. They don't get it. Just look around you. Ask yourself if you or any family member, relative, or friend owns a foreign car. Look at all your cell phones and audio, video, and computer equipment. Look again at Christmas decorations, clothing, appliances, and household items. For every one you identify as made in "someplace other than the U.S.A.," count yourself as a contributor to the export of jobs. Ask yourself why you chose to purchase an import rather than a domestically produced product. Once you have answered these questions honestly, then you can begin to understand why and what we need to do.

We still have time to right the sinking ship. The solutions are not always straightforward, and they are the result of integrated implementations of unconventional thinking and the will to accept these notions and programs. The desire to succeed will also require that we discard some very ingrained traditional concepts. Some may be radical and some may be hard to accept, but reality in the end will dictate success or failure. The pain incurred in achieving success will be great, but nothing compared to that of failure.

An example of the type of solution necessary for our auto industry to become more competitive again was the announcement by GM (this was during 2008), stating that they are offering a cash buyout to the remaining 74,000 hourly employees if they will retire immediately and completely sever all financial ties to GM. As reported, the average employee makes approximately $28 per hour in wages. Including benefits, that figure rises to approximately $78 per hour, with an annual cost for wages and benefits totaling around $162,000 (as reported in the news). It was also stated that GM's foreign competition faced only about one third the labor cost for wage and benefits. GM would replace those retiring with new hires at a much-reduced wage and benefit structure. In February 2009, GM and Chrysler came back to Washington, D.C., to beg for a second helping of U.S. taxpayer bailout. Two years from now (in my opinion) neither company will be around in the same capacity they are now (that is if they are still around). The U.S. government, by taking a stake in these companies via the bailout, will soon dictate the product to be manufactured and marketed by these companies. Hybrid and all-electric vehicles are all the rage of Washington and the environmentalists. Politics will dictate what is produced as opposed to what the public really desires.

As I am writing this in early 2009, the country is in the throes of an economic recession, with unemployment rising precipitously. President Obama, has just announced his plan for increasing taxes on the wealthy to the tune of $1 trillion+ over the course of ten years. We have just signed into law a stimulus package worth around $800 billion, a bailout of the financial industry of over $1 trillion, and have plans for spending $460 billion for healthcare reform. Where is all this money coming from? It will have to come from higher taxes, and not just from the wealthy, but from everyone. It will also probably raise the rate of inflation and devalue the dollar. The cars that are going to be produced aren't going to cost less, especially if they will be fuel efficient hybrids or electrics; they will undoubtedly cost at least as much or more than they do now. Who will be able to afford them?

The same elected officials from the auto producing states, who along with auto industry lobbyists fought standards tooth and nail, are now demanding bailouts and fuel efficiency. Now government will be "pseudo running" the automakers, and that is precisely why they will probably fail, or at the very least never again regain their prominence. The transition from oil to hybrid over the long run is appropriate for many reasons. To mandate it in such a short time frame is a recipe for disaster.

From an environmental standpoint, battery power is probably more toxic to the environment than internal combustion engines. The manufacturing of batteries uses tremendous amounts of energy and creates tremendous amounts of toxic pollutants. The recharging of batteries will depend upon the generation of electricity that in turn is dependant upon coal, oil, or natural gas. Clean energy, or electricity produced by nuclear power plants, isn't really "clean" either, since the byproduct is spent uranium, which is a radioactive disposal problem. Where is the benefit in the rush to implement a different fuel source? In the short run, there is none. It is simply politics. We should continue to use oil while at the same time increasing fuel efficiency. We should also invest in research for long-term implementation of alternative environmentally friendly fuel sources. Currently they are too inefficient, expensive, and environmentally unfriendly.

As of today (2/26/09), the UAW members of Ford seem ready to ratify a new agreement that gives up benefits in order to maintain wages and healthcare. This is a tremendous move never before witnessed. They will agree to this only because the alternative is "too frightening to contemplate." According to an article in the *Detroit News*, one Ford worker said, "We feel like we are over a barrel ... I want to retire from Ford. I don't even know if that's possible anymore. I want to keep working. I want to keep my job." If they really want to keep their jobs, they will have to take bigger cuts and give back more still. Only then will they begin to become competitive again. I said it before and I will repeat it again. Until unions come to their senses and decide to live in the here and now by cutting wage and benefit demands to a competitive level commensurate to the skill level appropriate for the job, more jobs will continue to be "lost."

Here's another example of what I feel is American stupidity. The Boeing Company, which has a multiyear backlog of orders for aircraft, including the new 787 Dreamliner, is a victim of a strike by the machinists union. The union has demanded a pay increase of 11% over three years, job security, and the elimination of third-party contract work. The union representing Boeing's engineers has also gone on strike. To put things in context, the economy is in the dumper, unemployment is on the rise, oil prices have doubled in the last year, airlines have retired many inefficient planes and scaled back routes, and Boeing's chief competitor Airbus is taking market share away from Boeing. Boeing is reportedly losing hundreds of millions of dollars a week in penalties for failing to meet delivery dates.

This is all happening at a time when people are happy to still have a job, much less a salary increase. In my opinion, the unions are totally unrealistic in their demands, are crippling the future of the company, and will end up in the long run losing jobs to competition worldwide. It is sheer stupidity and a lose/lose situation for all. History is repeating itself.

As an update, Boeing has indeed been forced to layoff workers as many orders have been cancelled due to economic conditions. As long as a duopoly like Boeing and Airbus exists, there will never be an urgency to address labor costs and implement efficient production methods. It may take many years for serious competition to develop, but if it does, Boeing may end up being on the outside looking in and more American jobs will be lost.

What we need to do is implement a comprehensive national policy that fosters the rebuilding of our core industrial capacity and technological prowess. We can regain our leadership as the most powerful economic powerhouse the world knows. The solution requires a formula that may appear to be complex, but is rather simple in nature. It requires the integration of a new innovative education policy (see Chapter 10: Education), coupled with a revised tax code that is business friendly, and finally a national energy policy that makes common sense and that will promote future alternative fuels, independence from foreign sources, predictable costs, and reliable delivery infrastructure to support it. The United States of America can out-compete anybody; we just need to be more flexible in our business models and vastly improve our education models and support, rather than punish the entrepreneurial spirit of our citizens. The following chapters will provide the insight necessary to accomplish this.

Chapter 7

Trade Deficit

"I am not worried about the deficit. It is big enough to take care of itself."

—Ronald Reagan

I always remember Christmas morning at our house as I was growing up, in my preteen days. There are fond memories of trying to stay awake as late as possible on Christmas Eve, in the hopes of catching a glimpse of Santa Claus going about his business. It was a futile effort, as I always fell asleep before Santa arrived. Christmas morning ritual involved waking up and hurrying out to the living room to check and make sure that Santa had completed his rounds. Somehow, he never missed our house, as there was always a pile of wrapped packages surrounding the base of the Christmas tree. The ritual continued with getting ready for church, fidgeting through the service, and finally having breakfast with the family before retreating to the living room where we would be allowed to empty our stockings before my Father began to hand out the presents. It was at this juncture in life that I began to learn my first lessons in global economics. This is not to say that I was a budding Milton Freidman, Adam Smith, or Karl Marx, but I was unconsciously absorbing some basic economics.

The small trinkets assembled and stuffed in our stockings were always little toys made of tin. Inevitably, they were all stamped with "Made in Japan" on the bottom. The larger, more durable, quality toys, the wrapped ones, were stamped "Made in USA." As I grew a little older, the "Made in Japan" stamp on the trinkets was gradually replaced with "Made in Hong Kong," and cheap electronics, such as tape recorders, radios, and walkie-talkies, now bore the "Made in Japan" stamp. As I aged further, the progression continued with trinkets stamped "Made in Taiwan," cheap electronics stamped "Made in Hong Kong," and cameras, stereo equipment, and calculators stamped "Made in Japan." The progression continued as I got older with the stamps "Made in Singapore," "Made in Malaysia," and "Made in Thailand" all entering at the bottom of the food chain and working their way up, one step at a time. These stamps are noticeable on almost every item we hold in our hands. Some are visible, not by holding them in our hands, but rather by their names — Toyota, Honda, Nissan, Lexus, Infinity, Hyundai, Subaru, Suzuki, Mercedes, BMW, and Volkswagen, to name a few. Some things are less noticeable because we rarely see or think about them, like steel or oil.

Back in the good old days, when I still believed in Santa Claus, the names mentioned above, for the most part, didn't really exist, at least not here in the United States. We as a nation, manufactured, mined, and assembled almost everything that was sold in this country. Today, I am sorry to say, that is hardly the case. We have gone from a net exporter of products to a net importer of products. So? What's the problem with that you might ask? Isn't it true that Toyota and Lexus cars are far superior in quality, and on a relative basis cost less than American-manufactured ones, have a better warranty, and hold their resale value better? I would have to answer TRUE ... TRUE ... and TRUE.

From a consumer standpoint it certainly makes sense to spend your hard-earned money where you can get the best value, and chances are it is buying an imported product. While it may not be your personal fault that we as a country cannot compete with other countries' exports, it is nonetheless a problem. Every time we buy an imported product, we send our dollars overseas to the country that produced that good. It's true that not all the money goes to the producer, as the salesman, dealership, landowner, and dockworker are all employed or receive a cut as a result of the sale, but take a look at the Rust Belt, all those steel mills and factories now closed forever. The Big Three United States automakers are barely surviving companies. We have continuously exported our jobs and livelihoods overseas with our dollars. Why? Simply because we cannot compete on a labor cost basis. That is fact, and we must accept it.

We no longer live in a world where natural barriers such as oceans also serve as a protection against a hoard of less costly products. There is, however, a national security implication associated with this that I will address in a later chapter. We have not even seen the worst of this problem yet, as there are potentially massive economic powerhouses still to rise up. We have begun to see "Made in China" on just about everything, but there is still a long way to go before we feel the full impact of that powerhouse. Further out on the horizon is "Made in India," "Made in Russia," and still further out are all the nations on the African continent. Am I concerned? You bet I am! Should you be? YES you should! If you are currently ignorant of the future consequences, then you will become aware, for instance, when hit over the head with a two by four, namely gasoline at $15-plus a gallon.

I heard on the radio recently that we import almost 65% of our oil. China and India are already net importers of oil, and the countries of Africa will soon enough be net importers of oil also. As their economies grow, our oil needs will seem minuscule in comparison. There will be a limited supply of oil to go around, and simple supply and demand will dictate prices with the help of the OPEC cartel, of course. Basic economics will probably push oil to the stratosphere, say $200 a barrel. If you think our trade deficit is out of this world now, just wait until then. We as a nation, in order to survive the future and maintain our standard of living, must address the balance of trade issue.

The balance of trade issue, in my mind anyway, is more or less directly tied to the global economy. As technology advances by leaps and bounds every year, the world shrinks by just as much. When I say shrinks, I am not referring to a physical depletion of mass, but rather to travel and communication time. Today, a product can be designed and prototyped anywhere in the world and specifications for production can all be accomplished on a computer. These can be made available to anyone, anywhere with the click of a mouse. Distance is only relevant in terms of logistics, that is, freight and transportation cost for raw materials and finished product. We as a country must accept the fact that economics and economic models are no longer the same as they were even 20 years ago. Technology has become a great equalizer for even the poorest of nations. We are no longer competitive in many industries in which, only a short few years ago, we were dominant.

There are a couple of trade policy issues that I believe are critical to our survival. The United States is probably the most lucrative trading partner that any nation can have. As a nation, with close to 300 million people, we are a fairly large and prosperous country with a relatively high standard of living. Our markets are generally open to most nations and serve as a primary source of trade to these nations. Free and fair trade between nations enhances the lives of all who take part. On those nations we believe to be fair and good trading partners, we bestow the special status of most favored nation. This rewards those nations with fewer trade restrictions. I believe that we have granted most favored nation trading status too liberally, oftentimes solely in anticipation of a fair expected outcome, or for misguided political considerations. If the playing field were level to everyone, then it wouldn't matter; however, all too often I feel we are taken advantage of too easily.

While I was growing up, I can remember endless stories about how difficult it was for American manufacturers and exporters of goods to gain entry into the Japanese market. Cars, rice, oranges, and beef come to mind as examples of products that couldn't be moved off the Japanese docks due to restrictions of one nature or another. What it all boiled down to was a Japanese protectionist policy hindering fair trade. Meanwhile, Toyota, Datsun, Sony, Panasonic, Sharp, Casio, Nikon, and other Japanese manufactured goods couldn't be moved off our docks fast enough.

Today, we are dealing with China as a major source of imported goods. The Chinese have a policy that states that American manufacturers cannot set up a factory in China unless we partner with the Chinese and we cannot own more than 49% of the operation, yet we import limitless amounts of Chinese-manufactured products and have accordingly piled up a tremendous trade deficit with China. While it has not necessarily become a one-way street as far as trade is concerned, China definitely has the advantage. I say not necessarily, because, to a large extent, our standard of living has benefited from the availability of less expensive (and from a quality standpoint) sometimes-cheaper goods. The question is, at what cost? Your initial reaction is probably akin to anger at the Chinese and our politicians for allowing all the manufacturing jobs that produce these goods to be off-shored/out-sourced. We not only send our dollars to China, but we also send our manufacturing jobs there, too! Whoa! Hold on there!! We have been doing this since the end of World War II. The magnitude just gets larger every year. See the chapter "It's the Global Economy, Stupid!" to get a better understanding of the economic fundamentals of this issue.

What we as a nation need to realize is that this tidal wave of imports from China is still in its infancy stage. The Chinese economy is currently running at full steam and for the most part only a small percentage of their billion-plus populace is even participating in the game. Once you travel 100 miles inland from their coast, you begin to realize how vast their land is and how little of their country is actually living in the current century. This will change, and it will continue to change for the next 100 years. Along with this change, will also come revolution, in the economic sense anyway. As the populace gradually integrates itself into the real world, the rapidly increasing standard of living achieved by those involved in the economic expansion will continue to drive the desire for more and better quality goods and services.

Pressure will also build from increased demand for higher wages, and the rebirth of American-style unionism may eventually take hold. By this time, the Chinese brand of government will be under severe pressure to conform to the global economic system called capitalism. If the Communist government of China wants to survive in the global capitalist economy, they will out of necessity have to learn how to play nice with their trading partners. China will for a very long time be a major exporter of manufactured goods, but for just as long, they will need to be a major importer of raw materials and natural resources. The Chinese will also have to import quality luxury goods to satisfy their increasing upwardly mobile middle and upper middle classes. This is a key to our future success in restoring our competitiveness. Currently, we cannot compete with the Chinese from a manufacturing standpoint due to tremendous wage disparities. This will continue to put us at a disadvantage in the manufacturing sector. China and other currently undeveloped countries will continue to be the world supplier of manufactured goods until wage parity or some other force changes the dynamic.

In 2007, former Treasury Secretary Henry Paulson concluded two days of trade talks with Chinese Vice Premier Wu Yi, along with 15 Chinese ministers. At first glance, the results did not seem to be encouraging, but therein lies the difference between two vastly different cultures. In our culture, we want and expect no less than instant gratification, whereas the Chinese move at a pace slower than a snail. You would constantly be checking your "six," too, if there were billions of potentially unhappy people you had to answer to for a mistake. However there are a number of additional factors that we have to take into account when dealing with the Chinese. Culture plays a very significant part in the way they deal with others. The Chinese were very aware of U.S. unhappiness over their undervalued currency. We think that the Chinese have purposely kept their currency undervalued in world markets to maintain a great competitive price advantage over competitors. This keeps their exports priced low and ours expensive relative to both domestic markets. If their currency was allowed to float based on pure market forces, it would inevitably appreciate and their exports would become more costly, less competitive, and possibly less desirable, resulting in a loss of market share and a decrease in their trade surplus. The United States would prefer to see their currency rise in value to help level the playing field.

The delegation that came to the U.S. is the largest the Chinese have ever sent anywhere. This in and of itself should tell us how important they regarded this round of talks. They knew this would be confrontational, and if there is anything they least desire it is confrontation. They are skilled negotiators and they do not respond well if they feel threatened by our demands. They cannot allow themselves to appear to lose face in negotiations.

As a result, they told us that the reason that our trade deficit is so great is our appetite for their products, and that there is no one to blame but ourselves. They also let us know that they are not about to let their currency float, because it would harm their domestic economy and policy. They also not so subtly warned us against instituting protectionist policies or starting a trade war. They basically snubbed their noses at us and told us to take a flying leap. They probably felt comfortable doing this because they were dealing from a position of strength. They are well aware of the political divisions within this country and knowing at the time that there was an unpopular lame duck president (George Bush) with a host of major unresolved domestic and foreign issues only emboldened them. We appear to be a very weak nation to them, and in their way of thinking they could not possibly give us any meaningful concessions, appropriate or not.

During the previous round of talks, we brought to the table the issue of intellectual piracy. Their snail-paced reaction, to our request in the last round regarding piracy of intellectual property was a limited crackdown. This in no way was up to our expectations. In the U.S., as in most other nations, intellectual property rights such as patents and copyrights are respected, both from a legal and financial point of view. Use of these rights requires compensation to the owner of these rights. This is an acknowledged and agreed upon doctrine of the World Trade Organization, and violation thereof is akin to theft of services. This is a very serious issue, and the Chinese need to be very deliberate in enforcement of these rights within their country. I'm not sure that they comprehend just how important an issue this is to us. If they do not attack infringements in their own country with greater resolve, I propose preventing import from China of any product containing or used to facilitate use of any pirated intellectual property, until compensation for such is paid to those owed. If all audio and video related equipment, from cell phones to radios and iPods, were no longer allowed to be imported, the Chinese might take notice. While this is a drastic step, and would probably be viewed by the Chinese as a threat, it should be put on the table and implementation not ruled out.

Other countries, such as the oil producing nations of OPEC and Russia, due to their extensive ownership of the greater portion of the world's known oil reserves, will hold us over a barrel (pun intended) for the price of oil, continuing to drain our balance of trade dollars. If you feel despair at this point, join the host of our elected officials who probably recognize the same thing, but haven't a clue what to do about it other than to investigate the Big Oil companies for price gouging. They are professional politicians whose only ideas and policy proposals are those sniffed from the wind of their constituencies. Unless prodded with a high voltage cattle prod, they will not, with any conviction, stick their collective necks out and offer any sort of policy to rectify the issue.

All right, now you are really depressed, right? Hark, all is not lost. OPEC is a cartel, and serves its purposes by keeping the price of oil at an artificially inflated price. While we pay three plus dollars a gallon for gas (still not a whole lot), their populations pay pennies. There are a number of ways we can deal with this, but it will take the resolve of the American people to make it happen (see the chapter on Energy Policy).

Under United States law, cartels are illegal. Yet we still deal with OPEC on a daily basis. Why? Because we have to. In the interest of reducing our foreign trade deficit, I propose that we organize and legalize export cartels. Here is some food for thought, again a hair-brained idea, but nonetheless something outside the box. Given some real consideration, maybe it's even feasible.

How about an agriculture cartel? What is one of the most efficient, productive, and easiest ways to expand industries in the United States? Agriculture. Why don't we organize a cartel of OGEC — Organization of Grain Exporting Countries and index the cost for a bushel of wheat, barley, corn, and other grains to the cost of a barrel of oil? I can hear the howls of laughter already, but on a serious note, this is the type of thinking needed to compete more competitively in a global economic world and balance the trade deficit.

In 2007, OPEC warned that if we started substituting ethanol and other alternative fuels for gasoline, hence driving down the demand for and subsequently the need to import oil from OPEC, they would cut production and raise the cost of a barrel of oil to maintain their revenue stream. That is a big fat screw-you to the United States! This comes directly from our supposed friends and allies. I wonder just what our enemies are planning. I say $65 for a barrel of oil, then $65 for a bushel of wheat! This applies to exports only. For domestic consumption, we should be inclined to make food as inexpensive as possible, say $1 for a bushel of wheat. Let the exports subsidize the domestic; after all, this is exactly what the OPEC countries do with oil. If they don't like it, let them eat and drink their oil! We need a very serious energy policy that will totally eliminate our dependence on import of foreign fuels, and we need it fast!

Recently, I heard a disturbing report on Bloomberg Radio that stated: about 96% of all cars sold in South Korea are manufactured in South Korea. I will freely admit that I have not investigated the reason for this and any judgments would be pure speculation at this time. However, this points to a problem that needs serious attention. While I do not know what our balance of trade with South Korea is, I do know that South Korea, via Hyundai and Kia, are selling an increasing number of cars in the United States each year, and probably a whole lot more than we are selling of U.S. manufactured cars in South Korea.

There is probably a very good reason for this, such as the quality of Hyundais has gotten better and better each year, and from a pure value standpoint, they beat American manufactured vehicles hands down. Hyundai also built a major state of the art manufacturing facility in Alabama. As with other foreign automakers that are "eating our lunch," they are investing in the United States via infrastructure and jobs, somewhat offsetting the negative economic and psychological effects of the balance of trade and our deficit. While this offset somewhat tempers my anger, my pride and spirit remain very dented.

American cars used to be the standard that the entire world aspired to achieve. Travel around the world today, and you see very few American cars on foreign roads. We can no longer compete on either quality or affordability. Why? If foreign manufacturers can establish facilities in our own backyard, outsell our domestic brands, and still turn a profit, we need to do some serious soul searching if we are ever to reverse the trend. We as a nation need to do some root cause analysis to determine where the problem lies. I suspect it all begins with our implementation of state of the art technologies, labor issues, and trade policies. We have to examine all and make the tough decisions necessary to reestablish our competitiveness to reduce our trade deficit. Trade is necessary to acquire what we cannot manufacture, grow, or mine within our borders. It is also necessary to acquire our wants specific to our individual tastes and desires. Trade, out of necessity, also needs to be fair and balanced. If it is neither, we end up on the short end of the stick, jobless, in debt, and eventually powerless to determine our own destiny, because countries that hold our debt, such as China, will forever be able to dictate and hold sway over our policy and economy. Wake up America!!!!!

Chapter 8

Energy Policy (E=mc^2)

"All the waste in a year from a nuclear power plant can be stored under a desk."

—Ronald Reagan

L et me begin this chapter with a little historical background and situational awareness. First of all, the only energy policy that this country ever had was based upon the three pillars of oil, coal, and nuclear energy. In the beginning, during colonial times, wood was the primary fuel used for heating and cooking. Whale oil and candles provided light. As our country grew and the demands for a more efficient and appropriate source of fuel to run our factories became evident, coal fit the bill. Coal was relatively cheap and plentiful, but it had drawbacks, too. The logistics, mining, transport, and distribution, were, to say the least, cumbersome. Burning coal was also a very dirty proposition. Pollution, both air and water, did not even enter into the equation.

With the discovery of oil and associated distillates such as heating oil, diesel, gasoline, and kerosene, a new era of usage was ushered in, mainly for transportation. While coal was a staple for running the railroads, diesel was considered a much-improved alternative. The internal combustion engine allowed for mass production and ownership of automobiles. Air transport also became a viable means for travel and freight transport. Sailing ships and coal-powered steamships made way for diesel-powered ships. From the 1920s until today, little has really changed.

After WWII, nuclear energy was thought to be the way of the future. While nuclear energy was very cost effective, it too had drawbacks. Radioactivity and disposal of spent fuel were major concerns. Despite the assurances of the nuclear industry and government, the overall populace was not exactly convinced of the safety factor, especially when we knew of the power displayed by the use of the atom bomb. Three Mile Island scared the crap out of us and if that wasn't convincing enough, Chernobyl sealed the deal. Plans for nuclear power generation in the United States became a fantasy despite the safety assurances issued by a host of agencies and government officials.

There was always oil anyway, we all knew that it was cheap, efficient, and would never run out. Enter stage left, the Arab oil embargo of the 70s. Talk about a major headache and wake-up call. No matter, it didn't last long enough to be anything but an unpleasant memory. The oil spigot was once again turned on and we went back to our normal everyday living. This country never foresaw a reason to doubt the ever-present, cheap, and plentiful supply of oil.

As we progressed through the years, the automobile became a necessity for American citizens. Our mobility depended upon it. As a result, our modern-day infrastructure — as opposed to Europe's — was never fully developed to support travel by any means other than air and auto. Air travel was utilized primarily for long haul, i.e., usually for distances greater than 500 miles or so. Even then, car travel was still more convenient, because public transportation availability was still haphazard and costly at best.

This country, due to inherent geography, lent itself to the comprehensive development of infrastructure for use by automobiles. The Eisenhower Interstate Highway System, built after World War II, paved the way for future extensive auto usage. Because our country is so geographically widespread, and travel between major cities proved difficult, the system was proposed to facilitate military movement of materials necessary to support a war or emergency effort. The original concept was conceived by Adolph Hitler and resulted in Germany's Autobahn. A by-product of this effort was a boon to the auto industry. Our travel preferences became so dependent upon autos that railroads, other than those used in urban areas to support daily commutation to and from work, almost ceased to exist. Freight movement by rail is still a viable option for long haul and for commodities such as coal, but inter-city movement of goods is primarily accomplished via truck.

Long haul passenger traffic is a thing of the past. It is no longer competitive with other means of travel for a variety of reasons, such as time, cost, comfort, and convenience. The infrastructure to support such travel has been mostly scaled back and long ago fell into irrecoverable disrepair from what it had been during its heyday in the 40s.

This country became addicted to petroleum as the primary fuel source and never gave a thought to any other source as a significant alternative. Power plants were either coal, oil, or gas fired, until nuclear energy became feasible. Once nuclear power became too scary a proposition, coal, gas, and oil remained a staple fuel source. Aside from some experimental but irrelevant projects, gasoline was the only fuel source for autos. Trucks, ships, trains, and airplanes depended upon diesel. Some trains were electric, but not long haul freight. Heating was oil or natural gas. Oil was king. Gasoline was cheap. Americans had a love affair with their automobiles.

Beginning in the 50s, horsepower or "muscle" was a primary desire. Six- and eight-cylinder engines were standard. With the introduction of SUVs, utility nudged muscle out of the way for desirability. At times it seemed that everyone in America owned a pick-up truck. The bigger, heavier, and more powerful a vehicle became, the greater the demand for it. Everyone needed off-road capabilities; four-wheel drive became standard. Hummers, converted military all-terrain vehicles, began production of passenger vehicles. Gas mileage? Who cared? Gas was cheap! At $20 a barrel and with no supply shortages, gas was an afterthought. No one ever thought that oil would double in price to $40 a barrel, or $80, or $120. Now we wonder if and when it will hit $200 a barrel or beyond. We were asleep at the switch and totally unprepared for what transpired.

What happened?

There are all sorts of reasons to explain why the price of oil jumped from $20 a barrel to $136 a barrel a few short months ago. I watched with amusement on the several occasions when the United States Senate held hearings to determine the answer to this question. Americans began to feel pain when gas hit $3 a gallon after Hurricane Katrina wreaked havoc on the Gulf of Mexico. Oil drilling platforms suffered some short-term damage and refineries in Texas suffered long-term damage, which disrupted the flow of gasoline to U.S. consumers. We had to import gasoline from other countries until repairs were made to our oil infrastructure and the flow of gasoline returned to normal. It should be noted that due to environmental policies and government regulations, which make it extremely difficult and costly to build oil refineries in this country, we now have a severely limited ability to refine crude oil. We wondered how such a single storm could cause such a major disruption in production capabilities and raise prices so quickly. This if nothing else should have served as another wake up call to the illogical dependence upon oil and the fragility of our supply system.

Let's just think about where the oil we use comes from. When I say we, I am including the entire world. Our first thought is naturally that the countries of the Middle East (Saudi Arabia, Iran, Iraq) are the major sources, along with some other contributing countries. The reserves in Saudi Arabia are a closely guarded secret. Suspicion indicates that the oil fields are beginning to become depleted, as production is falling off, and more difficult methods of extraction are beginning to be implemented. Iraq is still nowhere near full production capabilities, but is gradually making progress in increasing the output. As stability returns to Iraq, greater progress is expected. Iran is producing as it always has, but maintains absolutely no refining capabilities. Stability in the Middle East is an oxymoron, and if we are foolish enough not to factor this in our energy policy, shame on us!

In Africa, Nigeria and Libya are the primary sources. Nigeria is constantly under threat of military and political instability and frequently curtails or shuts down production as a result. Libya only recently got back into the oil business, after the political and financial isolation caused by its leader's association with terrorism. In Europe, there is the North Sea oil field. This field has seen its heyday and is on the decline. Russia holds great promise with the proven reserves of its fields. But, political instability, an inhospitable environment, and lack of technical ability to develop the fields all contribute to current, less than stellar results. In South America, Venezuela and a recent large find off Brazil are the main oil sources. In Venezuela, President Hugo Chavez nationalized the oil fields, resulting in the expulsion and/or voluntary departure of the major oil companies who developed and maintained these oil fields. Consequently, Venezuelan production rates have fallen to less than 25% of what they were a couple of years ago. The find in Brazil is off the coast in deep water, almost two miles down. While the field is expected to be gigantic in size, the development will prove extremely difficult and production will not become a reality for a while.

Mexico is also a major producer and exporter, mainly to the United States. Mexico's oil reserves appear to be diminishing, as production is falling more and more every year. The Gulf of Mexico and offshore Cuba hold promise for large reserves and are beginning to be developed, but for political reasons, United States oil companies are prohibited from taking part in exploration or development.

The information that I have laid out before you is garnered solely from reading business publications and newspapers and by watching the various business shows on cable television. While I am not exactly an expert in this field, and this is only my opinion, I think we as a nation have enough sources of both oil and natural gas, both tapped and untapped, to serve our needs for the next century. The Marcellus natural gas field in the northeast, and other natural gas fields in the upper Midwest and southwest contain very large amounts of untapped natural gas. What we do not have is a comprehensive, strategic national energy policy governing how we consume, conserve, and develop our national energy needs. Without this, we will be forever tied to the whims of the dictators, megalomaniacs, and foreign entities that now hold all the trump cards. This can only lead to regional and world conflicts over control and access to natural resources. Have we learned nothing from history? If you have forgotten, then please read up on world history pre World War II.

Let's again take a quick look around the world at the sources for oil, only this time focusing our sights on just how the U.S. is impacted. First is the Middle East, where we have three major sources, Saudi Arabia, Iraq, and Iran, with Saudi Arabia, our so-called friend and ally. Stop dreaming, the Saudis are friends of convenience only. They are Sunni, unable to protect themselves from predatory neighboring governments such as Shia-dominated Iraq and, most importantly, Iran, the dominant military powerhouse in the region.

We saved the Saudis' butts from Iraq once, and they chose to deal with us grudgingly, as long as we can protect them from being taken over by their neighbors. They are not our friends, make no mistake. They despise us and every aspect of our lifestyle. Our presence in their country is like salt in a wound. We threaten their way of life, especially their Islamic fundamentalist view of how life is to be lived. We are infidels, and in their view, the only good infidel is a dead one. Let us never forget, that their Madras, Islamic schools, teach hatred of the infidel and are the fertile recruiting grounds for future terrorists. It was Saudi Arabia that produced Osama bin Ladin and al-Qaeda.

The government of Saudi Arabia is openly a partner in the fight against terrorism, but that is more a matter of self-preservation and show than anything else. That same government is suspected of covertly funding the Madras to prevent internal uprising and revolution. I expect that, the minute we exit the region, the Kingdom of Saudi Arabia will fall prey to Islamic fundamentalists, on the model of Iran. Internal unrest makes the production and pipeline facilities of Saudi Arabia extremely susceptible to terrorist activities. Let's face it, the only reason we are so-called friends, is due to their vast reserves of oil. If it weren't for oil, neither they nor we would give a hoot about each other. This is a marriage of convenience only. Oil supply from this country will always be a risky proposition.

Iraq is a potential future major source of oil. I say potential and future because the political instability of that country at this time is well-known. The future stability will totally depend upon the will of the people, both Iraqi and American. If the U.S. has the willpower to remain in Iraq and through our continued presence foster increasing stability, then oil output will increase back to normal levels and we may eventually be repaid for our efforts with favorable oil contracts and concessions. Realistically, I don't envision that happening; rather what I foresee is our eventual exit from that country once the government is stabilized. Upon our exit, Iranian influence, providing there is not a political populist citizen revolt in Iran, will dominate regional politics, with Iran eventually assuming control of Iraq. The Iraqis will concede power willingly, and Iran will seek to consolidate power over the entire Middle East. Don't count on Iraqi oil as a steady secure source of future supply. Iran does not like us and unless there is another revolution that results in a pro-U.S. government, I do not have hopes that Iran will be doing us any favors as far as giving us preferential treatment for oil supply. The possibility of Iran as a future source of oil supply is fragile and tenuous at best. The country will most likely remain outright hostile to us and unless economics dictate a mandate to trade with us, the Iranians won't.

All of these potential sources of oil supply produce a "sour" crude, that is, a high sulfur content that requires more refining to produce useful distillates. It doesn't matter, as the future for a continuous reliable supply is doubtful at best.

The countries of Kuwait and the United Arab Emirates are also suppliers friendly to the U.S., but absent our military presence in the region, they too will go the way of Saudi Arabia. Iran holds the key to the major chokepoint in the world, the Straits of Hormuz. Should they choose to close it, there would inevitably result a military conflict, whose outcome would probably cause a major disruption of oil supply for a very long time. Nigeria, which produces a "sweet" crude, is constantly embroiled in a militaristic political battle with insurgents. Antigovernment forces continually disrupt supply. The government is not strong enough to guarantee steady supply.

At this time, Libya's oil production capabilities are not yet developed, and while potential for large-scale supply is judged to be good, I am not optimistic about the future due to political instability throughout geographic region.

Near Middle East countries, such as Kazakhstan, Azerbaijan, and the neighboring countries, have shown potential as recent finds of oil and gas reserves of some magnitude may be developed fully. But, once again, due to geographics, pipelines for export need to cross national boundaries as there is no seaport for easy access. Another factor is the decidedly negative influence of Russia exerted upon these governments. Russia has exhibited an anti-U.S. stance, and for political and/or military reasons does not want a U.S. presence (in the form of big U.S. oil companies developing these fields) in this region.

Russia itself has enormous proven reserves in Siberia, and has previously welcomed U.S. companies with their technological know how to come in and help develop these oil fields. The climate is extremely harsh and the Russians lack the technology to develop these fields on their own. U.S. major oil companies did so, but it appears that Vladimir Putin has had a change of heart. He has consolidated power and seems to prefer the ways of the old Soviet Union. He has nationalized the private Russian oil companies and via trumped-up environmental charges reneged on contracts with the U.S. major oil companies. Since their expulsion, production rates at these fields have steadily declined. Putin also laid claim to the sea bottom of the Arctic in an effort to dissuade other countries from exploration and development of suspected reserves in this area. The rest of the world has dismissed this claim as having no basis, but time will tell how serious he is when other countries begin to show real interest. Regardless of what the future may bring, the immediate prospects of Russia as a friendly, steady reliable source of supply are far from good. The North Sea oil fields, I am afraid, have seen their better days. Declining production amidst harsh climatic conditions is not very encouraging for future prospects.

Let's now shift our focus to South America. Venezuela, which has always been a primary source of supply, is now questionable. One of the world's favorite megalomaniacs, Hugo Chavez, has become infected with self-importance. Though proclaiming democracy, he has steadily usurped the freedoms of his countrymen and assumed a dictatorial presidency. The more power he assumes, the steadier his country declines. He has fashioned himself as the Castro of the Latin hemisphere. He is a legend in his own mind as well as a two-bit thug. He also has nationalized the oil companies and basically thrown out the multinational major oil companies that kept his fields producing at full capacity. As a result of his policies, the field's production rates have steadily and drastically declined. Oil exports are his primary source of trade and income. With the decline in production also comes a serious decline in income. He can no longer deliver on all the promises he made to the other dictators in training of South and Central America, let alone his own country's people. Rampant inflation and a scarcity of consumer goods and food are becoming a very serious problem. It will only be a matter of time before the citizens of his country ungraciously remove him from power, recall the multinational oil companies, and restore normalcy. In the meantime, oil supply from Venezuela will remain tight.

Brazil, which is currently not a source of oil supply but an exporter of ethanol, has recently discovered a vast reserve of oil in coastal waters. While this is a significant find, it lies in water two miles deep and will prove both costly and time-consuming to develop. As a future source of supply, it may prove promising, but it contributes nothing to our current world supply problems.

Within the coastal waters of Cuba in the Gulf of Mexico, less than 90 miles from our coast, leases for exploration have been let to bid. Multinational majors, including the Chinese National Oil Company, have signed on, but due to our political policies, U.S. majors are prohibited from taking part. Reportedly, geological reports indicate substantial potential of reserves present. When Fidel finally kicks the bucket, his brother Raul will hopefully see the light and succumb to the pressures of the Cuban people to embrace democracy. If he doesn't, I fear for his longevity. When this happens, the U.S. will change policies and embrace the Cuban nation as an extension of our own country. Normal relations will be restored, massive aid and assistance will flow forth, Cuba will become the preferred backyard vacation paradise of the U.S., and our majors may get their fair share of the pie. But once again, though Cuba may prove promising as a future source of supply, it contributes nothing to our current domestic supply.

Mexico, another of our primary sources of supply, has begun to see its production rate decline. I am not sure as to the reason, whether it is exhaustion of reserves or failure to implement technological improvements to maintain extraction. Whatever the case, we should be partnering with the Mexicans to fully develop their potential as a country and in the oil industry.

In North America, specifically Canada, lie the largest reserves of tar sands in the world. The province of Alberta is the home to these reserves. The extraction process is extremely costly in both development of infrastructure and ongoing operations. The climate plays a major limiting factor in development, as work can only be done during the summer months. Lack of pipelines to refining facilities inhibits the transport of extracted and processed product. Oil prices have only lately made the development of these reserves a viable option. It will be years before they become a factor in the world supply of oil, assuming oil prices remain at very high levels. In the United States, all easy sources of extraction were depleted years ago. Recent finds in the upper midwestern states may prove beneficial, but supply is years away. Natural gas finds in this area, some western states such as Colorado, and the Marcellus areas of southern New York and Pennsylvania may become significant sources of natural gas supply in the future. In Alaska, Prudhoe Bay is in decline, and known reserves in ANWR (Alaskan National Wildlife Reserve) are untouchable due to environmental politics.

It should become obvious even to the casual observer that global sources of oil are fraught with obstacles either political or natural, which constantly threaten the world's steady supply. We recently witnessed dramatic volatile surges in the price of a barrel of oil. It had risen as high as $136 per barrel, but currently resides at $77 a barrel as of 1/22/10. While the price is lower than it had been, it appears that the sky is the limit, depending upon supply. Supply is currently just keeping up with world demand; however, growing demand, especially from the emerging countries such as China, India, and Russia will most likely outstrip supply in the future.

Consider just this fact alone: In the United States, where there are some 300 million people, there is something like 800 cars for every 1,000 people. In, China where there are more than 1 billion people, there are only about two cars per 1,000 people and somewhat the same ratio applies to Russia and India. In Africa, the ratio is even lower.

China and India's economies are expanding rapidly. As a result they are both developing middle classes with consumer desires that were heretofore absent. The demand for consumer goods and the ability to afford them is a new reality for these countries. In China, autos are in greater demand every day. India will soon begin production of a very affordable small car for domestic consumption. The demand for oil is going to skyrocket.

Now consider this: It will probably take another ten years before the economic expansion even begins to affect a quarter of these populations. When the economies of Russia and the countries of the African continent begin to expand as is expected, demand for oil will surely outstrip supply. Russia already has proven reserves in Siberia, and claim to the Arctic Ocean floor anticipates the need for a longer-term supply source. Neither India nor China have much in the way of proven reserves and will need to import much of their supply. China, however, during the past few years has been purchasing the development rights and acreage leases for oil reserves throughout the world, especially in Alberta, Canada, where it has acquired vast areas of tar sands. Both China and Russia are anticipating future supply shortages and are already securing their sources. The supply of oil is not limitless and competition for scarce resources in the future could make for some eventful times. It would be better to stay on the sidelines and not be involved in any possible conflicts or tensions that may develop between countries in need of energy supplies. The best way to do this is to be energy independent.

What Are Our Options?

To this point, in reaction to the rapidly increasing price of gas, we sat back and enjoyed the show put on by our ineffectual Congress, as it held hearings to determine if the major oil companies amassed windfall profits. Our elected officials had to put on a show to demonstrate that they are aware of the problem and are reacting to it. I honestly do not think they fooled anybody.

John McCain called for a tax moratorium on gas during the summer months of 2008 to help ease the burden on the consumer. It amounted to a nice gesture at best. Don't hold your breath though. Forfeiting a tax revenue stream is not in the lexicon of Congress.

Barack Obama on the other hand, called for a tax increase on windfall profits. His logic, if that is what you want to call it, escapes me, as taking profit away from Big Oil via a windfall profits tax accomplishes nothing. Big Oil would simply pull up roots in this country and relocate elsewhere, where tax policy is friendlier. Without U.S. government restrictions, Big Oil could sell to anyone they want, and the price of gas could end up being $20 a gallon.

What would we do with these additional taxes anyway? Is the government going to cut a windfall tax rebate check to all citizens? Is the government going to start a "Government Big Oil" company of its own, or start an alternative energy company of its own? If these taxes are not directly returned to the consumer, there are no benefits to the consumer. Those who paid for this tax windfall in the first place, via gas purchase would end up shouldering the disproportionate burden of paying for this. The consumer who buys 1,000 gallons of gas a year would receive the same benefit as the consumer who only purchased 100 gallons. The person who doesn't even own a car has paid nothing into this tax, but benefits the most. This is a very scary mindset and follows Obama's call to eliminate tax breaks for the rich and redistribute to the poor. It smacks too much of socialism to me. This is not the answer to the problem. It may be change, but this sort of change is extremely shortsighted. Government has and never will be the best allocator of capital to solve economic or business problems.

There have been calls to open up the Strategic Petroleum Reserve to bolster supply and hopefully bring down prices. I believe this would be a big mistake. The Reserve is intended to counter a total cutoff of supply to our nation. It is a strategic reserve and should not be used for economic countermeasures. It must remain off the table as an option. John McCain had called for the opening up of offshore coastal drilling and then President Bush had called on Congress to allow offshore drilling in our coastal waters as well as in ANWR. The Democrats promptly pulled that bill from the table explaining that we cannot drill our way out of this. Instead, they have countered with possible legislation to regulate speculation in the oil commodities exchanges.

In response to Bush's call for drilling, the best that I heard was from some Democratic no-name Congressman or Senator from Illinois,

standing in front of the Democratic leadership for a nationwide broadcast, suggesting that the government nationalize the oil companies.
How in God's name do these people get elected? They're idiots! No
wonder we are in the situation that we are in. Our politicians can only
come up with half-baked, knee-jerk ideas to solve serious problems.
Calls had been made to remove the tariffs from the ethanol that Brazil
exports so we could use that in a blend of fuel (E85), but that suggestion
had fallen on deaf ears. I suppose that is due to the farm lobby whose
constituents (farmers) had benefited greatly from the tremendous
increase in the price of corn.

Unintended Consequences

The Federal Reserve was contemplating raising the interest rate to
combat inflationary pressures that could mainly be attributed to food-
and energy-price cost increases. We are our own worst enemy. Years
ago, after the 1979 Arab oil embargo, we should have mandated that all
vehicles that run on gas achieve a minimal standard of, say, 40 mpg.
Instead, we caved in to the auto industry, whose best selling and most
profitable vehicles were SUVs (trucks). Instead, we all wanted our SUVs
and didn't give a hoot about gas mileage. We mandated marginal
increases in mpg to be effective years from now.

Recently, our environmental conscience was eased with legislation
calling for incremental increases of ethanol to be blended with our gas
over the next few years. Ethanol in the United States is made from corn,
and as an efficient alternative energy source it is a bust! It requires tons
of corn to make meaningful amounts, tons of water to irrigate the corn
and process it, and lots of gas to farm it and transport it. Since there
was a shortage of corn to feed the ethanol processing plants, farmers
planted more acreage to corn, and less acreage to other grain crops.

Shortages in all grains have cropped up (no pun intended). Corn is a major primary ingredient in food processing and a major feedstock for cattle, poultry, and other animals. Shortages of corn have been a primary reason for the increases in food costs. We have gained nothing and paid dearly for our misguided ethanol adventure. Better to abolish the import tariffs on ethanol and import it from Brazil.

The following are some of the components I believe necessary to achieve energy independence. We also need to do a few things to prepare for the implementation of a long-term energy independence plan. We as a nation must admit to the fact that we are totally unprepared to deal with a future without oil. We must also take the politics out of the equation and stop blaming one party or the other for failure to be prepared for the current state we are in. The Senate and all politicians should stop grandstanding with their hearings where they grill oil company executives and accomplish nothing. Yes, the price of oil is crazy and partly influenced by speculation, but the oil companies whose profit margins are around 10% are probably not price gouging the public. Talk of implementing a windfall profits tax makes great headlines for elected officials who haven't a clue what really needs to be done, but should be dropped unless of course it is applied to every business in the country. If that happens, then we should also change our country's name to "The United Socialist States of America." It would better reflect our policies.

Where Do We Go From Here?

Let me take one example to portray the evolution of fuels as an energy source. One of our first sources of home lighting was the candle. Candles were replaced with better fuels such as coal gas, whale oil, and kerosene. With the perfecting of electricity and incandescent light bulbs, these were discarded or became secondary. Electricity became our preferred source, and various forms of lighting were invented. Fluorescents and sodium vapor lights came into use. Today, with the emphasis on conserving energy, incandescent light bulbs are being legislated out of use to be replaced with compact energy-saving fluorescents and LEDs. The right tool for the right job is a logical way to comprehend this evolution.

We have abundant fuel supplies to produce and satisfy our energy requirements. Some of these sources were curtailed or shelved due to environmental, political, or safety issues. Two major sources are currently out of favor: coal-fired power plants were responsible for acid rain, which destroys our forests, and high levels of carbon dioxide emissions, an Environmental Protection Agency–classified greenhouse gas. Nuclear power plants have not been promoted due to safety concerns and spent-fuel disposal issues. This is not to say that these sources should be prohibited from future deployment. The first thing we need to do is assess the current use of our fuels and try and determine the future course and needs of how we employ our sources of supply. Whoa. Now that's a mouthful! Translated, what it means simply is that we use the right tools and energy sources for the job at hand.

We have already seen how, in response to high gas prices and environmental concerns, hybrid automobiles took on a life of their own. I personally do not think that these are the answers, because the pollution and destructive means of production used to produce the batteries used in hybrids far outweigh any environmental benefit derived. However, it is a start and an awareness of our problems.

Honda recently introduced a hydrogen-fuel-cell-powered vehicle that is totally nonpolluting. What other environmental production issues are associated with this product I do not know, since I am not familiar with the fuel-cell production process. I would hazard a guess that this vehicle is very expensive and not yet at the stage where it is ready for mass consumer purchase. If it were, I am sure Honda would have lines of people out the door trying to get one. The important thing to note is that alternative sources of fuel production are being developed and implemented. In these cases, gasoline as the primary source of fuel is eliminated or decreased. This is an important step toward freeing ourselves from the stranglehold of the OPEC cartel and moving us closer toward energy independence. This is the same evolutionary path that the candles to electricity example represented.

We rely on oil as a fuel source to power far too many of our daily needs. But, some of these needs can only be satisfied by oil, at least for the immediate future. In the long term, many, if not most needs now powered by oil can be substituted by an oil replacement. Some, as in fuel-cell technology, may happen more quickly than others in response to market forces. Others may need the help of government via mandates, legislation, and long-term policy formulation. To be energy independent, we need to address how we as a nation use our fuels.

There are three primary uses of fuel sources: to generate electricity, to heat and cool our homes, and to power our transportation needs. Electricity is the essential lifeblood of everything. Just about all sources of energy supply are used to convert potential energy sources to electricity. We burn hydrocarbons to create heat, which we transform to steam, which in turn powers turbines to generate electricity. We also use hydro, solar, wind, uranium, and battery power to generate electricity. (We use these same sources to create controlled explosions to provide thrust, as in jet turbines or internal combustion engines. We use some of the sources to drive mechanicals, such as waterwheels and windmills, to power non-electric processes.)

We burn coal, oil, and natural gas, and harness nuclear energy to generate electricity via our power plants. We use that electricity to run just about everything in our homes. This is no stark revelation to any of us. How much electricity we use is only realized when we receive our monthly utility bill. What we do not realize is just how wasteful a user of electricity we are. Those of us who do not pay the electric bill tend to think that it is free and a God-given right to have unlimited access to it for anything our heart desires. This is evidenced by the number of lights that are left on when no one is in a room, by the number of charger devices and appliances such as computers that are left turned on and plugged in when not in use, the number of air conditioners left to run with the house windows wide open, or the TV or radio left on when there is no one around to enjoy the benefit.

Those of us who do pay the bills see how wasteful we are. We as a society tend to ignore calls for conservation, thinking that each individual cannot possibly contribute much. And that is only if we are even cognizant of conservation practices. I would be willing to bet that at least 30% or more of the electricity that we use daily is wasted. Nationwide, I bet that translates into a few thousand or hundreds of thousands of barrels of imported oil each and every day. That is just the waste!

With the ability to install solar electric panels (which I have done), electricity usage via the local utility company could easily drop by 50% or more. If every business and home in this country were to install these panels, we could probably curtail oil imports by hundreds of thousands of barrels a day. If we were to install solar water heating systems in all locations, the savings would be even greater. These solar systems are extremely expensive, I know through experience. However, there are many benefits to be derived from a long-term plan to migrate in this direction. Currently, there is about (at least for me), a 20-year ROI for these systems, not exactly where you want to invest your hard-earned money. If there were a mandate to convert to solar that was phased in over a ten-year period, there would be a known demand for these products.

Today, most solar panels are manufactured in other countries, especially China, and imported to the U.S. With a known demand, production and investment in better, more efficient technologies to greatly reduce the time to ROI would produce untold jobs both in production (manufacturing) and installation of these systems. Mandates that all new home construction require solar and energy efficient materials and systems would also spur research and development into cost-effective technologies employing storage batteries to enhance these solar systems. Business, due to known demand, would ensure a downward spiral in cost as efficiency of manufacture and design improvements would yield cost savings unheard of today. That's capitalism, doing what it does best! Let's call this the "Here Comes the Sun" initiative. This approach would serve light residential needs, and definitely decrease the amount of oil imports. For heavy needs, like commercial and manufacturing, utilities could also employ solar (some out west have already begun to do so) to supplement generation. Where this is not practical, we need to rely on more traditional means of generation. Here is where a joint effort between government and industry can be effective.

During World War II, the United States realized that the production of an atomic bomb was an absolute necessity to win the war. Franklin D. Roosevelt initiated the secret Manhattan Project where the top scientists available were assembled for the purpose of building the bomb in as short a time as possible. This was a monumental undertaking, since everything about nuclear science at this time was primarily theoretical. Due to the importance of this project, no expense was spared.

I propose that we endeavor now to initiate a series of projects in the name of energy independence, much in the same manner and urgency as the Manhattan Project. I envision three separate projects. Successful completion of any of them will greatly pave the way to energy indepen-dence; success of all would virtually guarantee it.

The first initiative should be to develop a cost-effective way to mod-ify coal for a clean burning solution. Coal is one of our most abundant natural resources and dollar for dollar in today's market place, one of the most cost-effective sources of supply for energy. If we can find a way to eliminate the pollution when burning it, then we will have an untold supply of fuel for the next 100 or so years. Just replacing oil with coal will go a long way in reducing our dependence upon oil imports. Coal can easily be used as a fuel supply for both power plants and heavy industry. With further technological advances that are sure to develop in the future, coal may even be relegated to a backup strategic energy supply. For now, however, a strategic goal should be to find a way to make it clean burning.

The second initiative, probably a good deal harder to achieve, is to take fusion from the theoretical to the actual. If we could do it with fission, then I believe with the right concentration and incentives, we can do it for fusion. A safe fusion process for creating another environ-mentally friendly and cost-effective source of energy production would also go a long way to free us of the OPEC bonds.

The third and probably most difficult initiative is to find a way to recycle the by-products of nuclear fission. If we could develop a process to safely use the radioactive properties of spent fuel to generate power, then nuclear power plants could become a tremendous source of electrical energy and the by-product could also be used for the same purpose. This truly would be the gift that keeps on giving. From an environmental standpoint, nuclear waste dumps could become a thing of the past. Expansion of the base of nuclear plants could become less contentious an issue. Technology for safer nuclear plants through science needs to become reality, not just a dream.

These three initiatives are long-term solutions and will do nothing quick to bring down the price of oil or grant us energy independence. In the meantime, we must continue to develop the more easily attained solutions such as solar, wind, fuel cell, and, yes, oil.

After 1979, when we first became aware of our vulnerability to the Middle East for oil supply, we fell asleep at the switch. We hoped it was all a bad dream and that it would eventually go away. To some extent, it did. It lay dormant for a few years, but recently awoke with a vengeance. We did not think outside the box as we should have, but rather went back to our old wasteful, but dependable, ways. We are beginning to make some headway toward the development of better ways to fuel our vehicles, but we still have a long, hard journey ahead of us.

Transportation, the second most intense use of oil will not be a quick fix. Electric cars and hydrogen fuel cells are alternatives, but even electric cars require batteries that need to be recharged. We are still tied into the grid for electricity, which needs to be generated by a more cost-effective fuel source to make electric cars truly viable. Storage batteries need to be developed that are environmentally friendly yet hold a charge for much longer periods of time. Once we have developed batteries of this nature that will sustain driving distances of 500 miles or more without recharge, then electric cars will be viable. Better batteries can also be used for other forms of transport, such as mass transit systems and marine transport.

Much development needs to be done before this is viable solution, but if we don't start, it won't happen. Air transport may prove to be the most difficult to power by anything other than petroleum distillates. Fuel cells could probably be used to power prop driven planes. These could be used for short haul or feeder routes to big hubs, where larger planes do the long haul, just as today. For long haul on large planes, jet fuel appears to be the only good fuel at this time. In the future, based upon the work of people like Richard Branson who has vowed to fly his Virgin Air fleet on environmentally friendly fuels, maybe a better solution will be developed. Warp factor one, Mr. Sulu?

President Obama, the Democrats, and John McCain are opposed to drilling off shore along our coasts, in the Alaskan National Wildlife Reserve. This is shortsighted. Sure, we are all aware of the environmental issues, but I think we have proved that we haven't killed off the caribou in Alaska by drilling in Prudhoe Bay, and Hurricane Katrina, as devastating as it was, didn't result in wholesale pollution of the Gulf of Mexico from oil-rig failures. The Democrats have stated that we cannot drill our way out of this mess. That is true, but we shouldn't bury our heads in the sand either. We need oil, now and in the future.

Whatever alternative fuels may come, we will still need oil for some things, especially in the near term. We must not forget that oil and natural gas are the building blocks for products such as plastics, man-made fibers, pharmaceuticals, and fertilizers. Without these products, we probably could not feed, clothe, or cure ourselves. These are products and byproducts derived from oil that are not used for energy purposes, but rather employed much as wood, copper, and other natural resources are. They are essential to our everyday living. Remember, our goal is to achieve energy independence and sever the chains that bind us to OPEC and other potential threats to our energy supply. We need to target our fuels and natural resources for the right use.

Let's take air travel for instance. Due to the tremendous price increases in the cost of jet fuel, air carriers have had to resort to cutbacks in service, in some cases eliminating service altogether to some smaller markets. Less fuel-efficient planes have been taken out of service to save on fuel costs. Cutbacks in workforces are occurring. Higher fares are beginning to be published, and charges for baggage have been implemented. Some carriers declared bankruptcy and folded their tents. Due to the geographies and distances between cities of this country, as opposed to European countries, air travel, whether for business or pleasure, is a necessity. The infrastructure to support other means of long-distance travel does not exist. High oil prices are the death knell for this industry. We cannot allow it to collapse. The economic impact of such a collapse would be devastating to this country. We have to find a way to guarantee a stable supply of jet fuel at a fixed price to the airlines. To do this would require a true partnership between the airlines, oil companies, unions, and government. This idea may sound crazy, but I think it has legs. Let's call it FLY U.S.

FLY U.S.

What are the oil companies' needs? They need a source of reserves. They need a profit. The oil companies claim that they are not gouging the public, that they are only making a 10% profit. OK, let's give them what they need. Let's give them drilling leases in the coastal waters and ANWR. In return, we (the government) require 50% of all recovered oil and we guarantee them a 10% profit on the oil they deliver. Cost should be well below market price, say $40 a barrel because the reserves are easily recoverable, speculation is eliminated, and 25% of the oil companies' take can be sold at market prices, thereby guaranteeing the oil companies an even bigger profit. The other 25% of the oil companies' take should be allocated to the U.S. consumer in the form of a give-back.

That 25% could be allocated in the following way. A small percentage of the government's oil take (2%) would be earmarked for the Strategic Petroleum Reserve, 10% would be reserved for military use, 70% would be reserved for civil aviation, and the remaining 18% would be reserved for the states where the drilling occurs.

Airlines (U.S. carriers only) would be allowed to bid on these fuel supplies, with the minimum bid being 1% greater than the federal government's cost, and any profits would be earmarked solely for the FAA ATC systems. Awarding of contracts would be based upon several criteria, including customer satisfaction surveys, percentage of filled seats, compliance with FAA safety issues, on-time performance, and overall safety and age of the air fleet. These components could all be weighted, with guarantees that are based on these ratings; top performers would not be shut out of the awards. Additional considerations and stipulations for the airlines might be that better than 51% of their fleet be of U.S. manufacture, indirectly pushing the benefits derived to the U.S. manufacturing sectors, supporting U.S. jobs. Because this would be a form of government support of the industry, there needs to be a quid pro quo for the quasi-guarantee of keeping airlines above water and providing steady employment. Labor contracts should be subject to arbitration to ensure that neither the management nor the labor force derive undo benefit from the price break on the oil. Labor must be prohibited from striking, in accordance with the Taylor Act, and arbitration and mediation via independent third party must be the rule.

The oil companies, in return for the privilege to lease, develop, extract, and sell this oil at the guaranteed profit margin, should be required to give back to the consumer as well. This could take the form of blending the take from these leases with other sources of supply to yield an average price of all sources. This cost savings needs to be passed back to the consumer in the form of lower prices at the pump for automotive fuels, at distribution hubs for heating oil, and at the airline reservation counter with special pricing for U.S. citizens. The GAO should watchdog and publish the accounting for these derived prices.

Sounds crazy and complicated? Maybe it is, but desperate times call for desperate measures and it is an idea, a framework to build upon. I picked the aviation industry as an illustration because it is vital to our economy and the least likely to benefit from the use of alternative fuels in the short term. This philosophical design could be applied to any strategic sector, for any type of fuel. I believe that through the development of alternative fuels and expansion of the means of electricity production (additional nuclear power plants, clean coal, fusion, and radioactive waste recycling initiatives, solar and wind power generation) within ten years this country could drastically reduce its need for oil. Future oil needs could be met through development of tar sands and exploitation of natural gas reserves. As our demand for oil gradually decreases over time, the price may also drop or it might not, as developing countries increase their use over time, but it will not affect us because we will have achieved energy independence.

Future Directions

We can see that with the decline in the demand for oil, the oil companies will definitely lose a good portion of their domestic market and possibly their world markets as well. What are they to do? I suspect that for a very long time their expertise will sustain their traditional business, just their markets will no longer be domestic. However, these companies have and will continue to amass billions in profit for a long time. Instead of buying back shares of their own companies as the most effective way to burn their profit, it's time they focus on business continuity. They will need to redefine themselves. In the future, they will no longer be oil companies, but rather energy companies. If they are at all smart, they will start to invest their profit in growing businesses such as solar and alternative fuel development. The shift away from oil to these alternatives will require massive amounts of capital infusion for infrastructure development, manufacturing facilities, raw material acquisition, and research and development.

Candle makers still exist, but we no longer depend solely on candles for lighting our homes. Electric utilities will be in for a total makeover as well. They will no longer be solely a power-generating company, but rather a supplier of infrastructure to support distribution, storage, installation, maintenance, and sales of energy-generating and conversion systems. The electric grid in this country is so antiquated, dilapidated, and unreliable that we are susceptible to total collapse and failure at any time. This is not only a service issue, but a strategic national issue as well (more on this in the Infrastructure chapter). There is vast opportunity for the farsighted utility CEO who knows how to think outside the box. For those without vision, your skills will probably still be needed in developing nations. Bon voyage!

Ultimately, the Democrats are correct. We cannot drill our way out of this, at least in the short run. It could take at least five years to bring these new wells online, but they are dead wrong and sadly mistaken if they think we should forego drilling in these places. At this time, over 70% of the public is in favor of drilling in the Arctic National Wildlife Reserve and offshore. This is probably a knee-jerk reaction to high gas prices, and once it is understood that drilling will probably not lower the prices at the pump either now or in the future, opinions will most likely change. The fact still remains if we want to be energy independent, even if we develop and deploy alternative fuels, oil will still be necessary. The oil companies should start to drill on the current unexploited leases on land, or they should be put up for rebid with expiration dates and guarantees from the awarded bidders that development begin within a specified time period.

We must realize that we are a very long way from achieving energy independence. If we begin to focus on the easy steps first, such as residential solar for electricity and heating purposes, and exploitation of the vast domestic natural gas reserves, this could all be accomplished while we await ANWR and offshore drilling to come up to speed. Expansion of nuclear power plants, developing efficient storage batteries, and drilling in ANWR and offshore are more difficult. They are considered midrange goals. Long-term goals are the three Manhattan Project initiatives — fusion, clean coal, and radioactive waste recycling.

Solar and wind power are key. The federal government should grant massive tax credits to both residential homeowners and commercial businesses to jump-start and encourage this implementation. These credits could be applied toward the purchase of American-made solar/wind systems only. This would increase investment in and development of a domestic solar/wind industry. Job creation would be extensive, and these companies would qualify for the investment purposes of funding social security, Medicare, and other government-sponsored initiatives or programs. This is a win-win for America. Solar/wind initiatives can be cost-effective with initial kick-start government help via tax incentives, and should be viewed as a short-term implementation.

Natural gas for fueling autos is another initiative that can be started immediately. Natural gas is both plentiful and cheaper than gasoline.

Other alternatives are longer term, but these initiatives must be started right away also. Increasing domestic supplies obviates the need to fill the coffers of foreign countries, provides jobs for our citizens, and moves us closer to energy independence. Remember, the longest journey begins with the first step. LET'S GIT 'ER DONE!

Chapter 9

Immigration Reform

L et me state unequivocally right up front that the border problems of our country rest in totality with the federal government. It is the federal government's responsibility to create policy to secure our borders. Post Columbus, America has always been, from origin, a land of immigrants. We have forever been looked upon as the land of opportunity. The reasons for coming here are many and they have revolved around escape from religious persecution, escape from political persecution, escape from famine, and freedom to pursue the American Dream. In New York harbor stands the Statue of Liberty with the famous inscription:

> Give me your tired, your poor,
> Your huddled masses yearning to breathe free,
> The wretched refuse of your teeming shore.
> Send these, the homeless, tempest-tost to me,
> I lift my lamp beside the golden door!

Beginning over 100 years ago, greater than 25 million immigrants have passed the statue in New York harbor on their way to the Ellis Island immigration center, as their American Dream began. They came from all over the world and they became us. These immigrants, our forefathers, were not necessarily welcomed. They weren't met by cheering crowds and gala playing bands. For the most part they were dirt poor, they were despised and discriminated against, they were taken advantage of, they were ridiculed, they took the most undesirable jobs, worked for the lowest wages, lived in poverty, and struggled to survive. Survive they did. Against all odds, they gradually integrated themselves into the melting pot called America, and we are their living legacy. Now we are engaged in a great debate testing whether the inscription on the Statue of Liberty will hold true.

I acknowledge that there are some major differences between yesteryear's policies and today's reality. The simple addition of the word "illegal" to immigrant turns all argument on its ear. I daresay that not many people paid any attention to illegal immigration until it became a political cause celebre post 9/11, and therein lies the rub. Pre 9/11 everyone turned a blind eye to the massive numbers of Latino immigrants who illegally crossed our southern border on a daily basis. Our southern neighbor Mexico was barely a functioning sovereign political entity. Widespread corruption, a dysfunctional government, and a cycle of neverending poverty were all citizens could look forward to. For the most part, many other Latin American countries and their citizens faced the same conditions and the same future prospects. It was only natural that they turned their eyes northward to the land of opportunity. With a wink and a nod, we grudgingly accepted these pitiful souls into our country. While our border patrol did its best to prevent these people from crossing the border illegally, it was truly a losing proposition, equivalent to plugging the hole in the dike with a finger. Our major concerns were to detect and prevent drug smuggling, gang activity, and criminals from entering the country.

Why did we turn a blind eye to these illegal immigrants? We did this exactly for the same reasons that we were happy to accept European immigrants over 100 years ago. They take the most undesirable jobs and work for the lowest wages. Migrant farm workers have been an institution in this country for better than 50 years. Toss aside the notion that these people take jobs away from U.S. citizens. Citizens of this country will not take these backbreaking, low-skill, low-wage jobs. On the contrary, citizens of this country depend upon these workers to abundantly fill our tables with food purchased at reasonable, affordable prices. Without them, we could expect to see major increases in the cost of our food. These illegals are not only taking farm jobs, but have also expanded into the service industry, such as fast-food businesses, landscaping, construction, less desirable factory work, and restaurant kitchen help, to name a few other types of employment.

The major issue that has evolved over the years concerning these illegals is the burden they have gradually begun to place on our health-care and school systems. We have over time created a sort of purgatory where they exist. They are happy to stay below the radar and remain as inconspicuous as possible, lest they be discovered and consequently deported. Their own government is happy to see them head north and actually encourages them to do so. This alleviates the Mexican government of its responsibility to support them with costly humanitarian services; that cost instead is shifted onto the backs of the U.S. taxpayer. At the same time, the illegals provide an income stream to the Mexican citizens as their earnings are sent back home to their poverty-stricken families. There is absolutely no urgency on the part of the Mexican government to put a halt to illegal immigration.

Again, the simple addition of the word illegal to immigrant is the major sticking point that argues for reform. We are traditionally a country made up of immigrants and we freely accept immigrants into our melting pot. Immigration must be accomplished legally for a variety of reasons. First of all, in fairness to all other nationalities and countries from which we accept immigrants (usually with annual quotas for people who have been accepted into this country and have become citizens), we need to apply some standards to those who cross our border illegally. Just as we issue student or work visas to those who arrive here through legal channels, we must do the same for those entering illegally across our southern border.

Secondly, national security is now a major concern. We must, for our own safety and survival as a nation state, know via positive identification who is in the process of crossing our borders, who has crossed our borders, and where they are. This runs totally against our traditional values of freedom in all ways, shapes, and forms, but we only need to recall the events of 9/11 to realize that the world is different than what it once was, and extreme times call for extreme measures. No ifs, ands, or buts about it.

Thirdly, the fiscal burden placed upon our social infrastructure by the illegals is costly, inefficient, and unnecessary. I have already railed against the costly tax burden placed upon us for supporting an inefficient education system in the Education chapter, but let me add to it here. It is costly enough to educate our own citizens, but to also support the education of noncontributing illegals is asking a bit too much. This support also extends to the local medical facilities, especially hospital emergency rooms that are required to treat all who enter regardless of ability to pay. Don't get me wrong; I am not a heartless individual who would deny any human being the necessities of life. I am just a very frustrated taxpayer who wants to see controls put in place to minimize the waste of tax dollars. There is a very humane way to accomplish this, if only our elected officials would stop playing politics and do their jobs.

Let's do some root cause analysis here. We have two very wide land-based borders in this country, one with Canada and one with Mexico. The border with Canada is much longer than the one with Mexico. Why are we not experiencing the same mass illegal immigration over our northern border as we see over our southern border? From an economic standpoint, there is poverty in Canada, the same as there is poverty in both the United States and Mexico. The existence and degree of poverty in both the U.S. and Canada are far less than that in Mexico. Improving one's economic and social status in the U.S. and Canada is more easily accomplished through hard work and education. The "dream" may not be achievable overnight, and may take generations to come to fruition, but the opportunity definitely exists. In Mexico, hard work is easy to accomplish, but education, especially at the higher levels, is far less available than in the U.S. or Canada. More than likely, a family living in poverty in Mexico will remain in poverty for generations to come unless they remove themselves from the surroundings that foster this cycle — hence the illegal migration to the United States. These migrants put everything on the line to improve their lot and their future generations' lot. Therein lies the difference between Canada and Mexico. Political stability is the major glaring difference between our two neighbors. Political stability fosters stable economics and achievable dreams, whereas political instability destroys them. Can we the people of the United States rectify this situation? It may take a long time to accomplish, but for all concerned, we must!

I will propose a possible solution. First, let's take a look at our current and past policies. Back when we were still a developing nation (not that we aren't still today), we gladly accepted immigrants, largely from Europe, who could fill our factories, till our soil, fill the ranks of our military, and homestead our western lands. An immigrant's level of education or size of bank account was not a high priority. We did maintain a standard of public health to prevent epidemics or widespread disease from taking a foothold in our population.

As our country has developed over time, we have taken on a more protectionist approach toward those we allow to enter. We have established quotas by country and also by skill set to limit any potential negative effect on our own citizens and their economic livelihoods. We also try to screen out criminal undesirables, and try to ensure that immigrants' economic status will not impose a hardship upon our own citizens or infrastructure. We tend to prize potential immigrants with high levels of education, and allow student and work visas to be given to people who are working toward or have attained higher education degrees. We are still a worldwide magnet for higher education. These potential immigrants all must go through legal channels to come here, and often have to wait years to be afforded this opportunity. On our southern border, due to proximity, politics, and economics, legal channels have become irrelevant. There are many issues to address and their resolutions need to be implemented in a phased approach.

The first issue is political. As long as the government of Mexico turns a deaf ear to the illegal border-crossing problem and even encourages citizens to do so, the issue will never be resolved. It will require a joint effort on both governments' parts to solve this problem.

During a book tour in this country, former Mexican President Vincente Fox stated very emphatically that the current Mexican government is addressing the immigration issue. The problem, as he sees it, is that the current political party in power, which is trying to address this issue, has only been in power for seven years, not a long enough time to affect the necessary change. We already know that the lack of opportunities to achieve their dreams is the root cause of illegal immigration for the citizens of Mexico, and the Mexican government, regardless of intention, appears helpless to rectify this. Therefore, the Mexican government needs help, and the United States needs to partner with our neighbor to modify behavior and their citizens' expectations. We have neglected our southern neighbor far too long, and the consequences have come home to roost. Mexico is a country rich in culture and resources, both natural and human. There is no reason why it is still such an impoverished nation state, while countries with fewer resources are prospering. Mexico has the necessary ingredients to be a truly developed and flourishing nation. The United States can help it achieve this goal. There are three main initiatives that must be undertaken to satisfy the requirements of transforming Mexico from poverty to prosperity: government reform, social reform, and economic reform.

Simply stated, the citizens of Mexico need to believe in the stability and honesty of their elected federal officials. This also applies to the local political levels. Corruption must cease to be an accepted way of doing political business. Elections need to be fair, and elected officials need to be held accountable for their actions (I must admit we in the United States still have not figured that one out). Corruption must be weeded out. A strengthening of the military, local law enforcement, and the Mexican justice system must be implemented to restore the average citizen's faith in government.

A major, seemingly unsolvable problem is the drug trafficking through Mexico and across the border, leading to a border rife with lawlessness and corruption. This is certainly a situation demanding a joint effort, possibly/probably involving the military and local law enforcement on both sides of the border to interdict, capture, and incarcerate the drug traffickers. This can only be accomplished with the total commitment of the Mexican government and a beefed-up Mexican justice system. The United Sates can provide training and leadership expertise to guide this process. We will also need to put our military (in force) on the border. This is the lynchpin upon which all else rests.

Social reform is critical to the sustenance and nurturing of a poverty-stricken population. Plans need to be developed for the building of infrastructure to support medical care, housing, water and electric distribution, waste management, educational facilities, and transportation systems. Without these basic necessities, dreams will whither and die on the vine. These improvements will take a lot of time, but they can be jump-started with United States help in establishing permanent medical missions, supported by reserving space in our medical schools for Mexican nationals who will return to their country to staff these missions. Infrastructure development and improvement can only be accomplished in conjunction with the rooting out of corruption at all levels of government. While this (infrastructure development), is a costly venture, it can be underwritten by the export of natural resources (mainly oil and copper), agricultural and manufactured goods, along with help from the World Bank and the International Monetary Fund. Additional training and educational efforts in areas of city planning and urban development can be provided with assistance from the United States. This will serve to prime the pump by providing employment opportunities for substantial numbers of the Mexican population. It will also serve to inhibit the flow of illegals across the border in search of employment.

Economic reform must go hand in hand with these other initiatives to affect a positive result. NAFTA has provided an opportunity to increase economic stimulus to the Mexican economy. If the Americans can work with the Mexicans to foster trade between the two countries, a stronger bond will develop, which will foster better policy and economic ties in the future. All of Latin America needs to become a stronger partner to the United States, and a successful partnership with Mexico can lead to better ties with all countries within our hemisphere.

This is a long-term solution and will eventually produce a mutual benefit for all involved. The short term, however, is an immediate problem requiring tough positions and commitments. The presence of millions of illegals within our borders must be addressed. I personally believe that these people represent little in the way of a national or economic threat to America. For the most part, they are hardworking, honest individuals who are not taking jobs from Americans. I also believe that it is in America's best interest, especially in the long term, to create a guest worker program. I also believe that since the border between our countries is very porous and poses a considerable threat to our national security, it should be closed. If this requires the construction of a wall with technological monitoring and detection devices, so be it. Minimally, the United States military must take up station along the border.

There is the sticky issue of what to do about all the illegals who currently reside here. This issue is compounded by the fact that many of these illegals have children born in this country during their stay here. This makes them a family of illegal parents with children of United States citizenship. A possible solution to this might lie in the guest worker program, along with legislation. Structuring a guest worker program in a way to provide business with guest worker wages (a minimum wage set at a lower level than the minimum wage, but requiring the business to provide healthcare benefits via a guest worker healthcare pool in return for the lower wage structure) would be the first ingredient.

Additional requirements might involve the illegal guest workers (with citizen children), to become U.S. citizens within a specified time period, providing they become fluent in English and have committed no other crime besides being here illegally. Once they become citizens, they are removed from the guest worker program. If they fail to become citizens, then they must be deported. If we were to allow business to hire illegals via a guest worker program, the guest workers would need to be registered with the INS via a guest worker database before employment. Business would be required to register with this same service as a participant employer of a guest worker. Failure to register with the program or hiring nonregistered illegals would result in revocation of participation rights (if registered), and stiff penalties per illegal worker on premises.

This concept would allow the INS to track the whereabouts of guest workers and the expiration time of their privilege, and to control of the number of guest workers in the program. This approach would also help alleviate associated costs on the medical system and social services, which is a major problem now. Legislation should be enacted to prevent the automatic granting of citizenship to children born to illegals and guest workers in the future. Any illegal who has, or is currently serving, in the armed forces of the United States, having been honorably discharged, should be given the right to become a United States citizen in return for their service. If they have any immediate family, then the offer should likewise be extended to them, provided of course they meet the same qualifications as any individual who is seeking to become a United States citizen. The United States military should be prohibited in the future from allowing illegals or any non-American citizen to serve.

The above-mentioned ideas are options; however, until such time as these options can be implemented, we are still faced with the real problem of what to do immediately. There is only one logical answer. We must first and foremost stop the flood of illegal immigrants from entering this country. We must bite the bullet and erect a fence that will enable us to secure our borders. The world has changed radically over the last decade and the consequences of not being vigilant and on guard could be catastrophic. Strong border protection requires a fence and the personnel to enforce our sovereignty. Drug smuggling, gang warfare, and possible terrorism are all very valid reasons to erect a fence and prevent illegal entry to this country. As distasteful as this may be to many people, the times have made it a necessity.

Chapter 10

Education

"There are no constraints on the human mind, no walls around the human spirit, no barriers to our progress except those we ourselves erect."

—Ronald Reagan

Disgusted with the annually increasing school taxes that you have to pay for the less than mediocre results gained? So am I! I cannot speak for the rest of the country, but I am appalled every time I hear or see the results of another survey of our high school or college students which has tested them on some of the most basic, even common sense things they should know, but don't. I may not have the exact questions or exact percentages of the resulting answers correct, as I did not record them at the time I read them, but I am pretty sure they are fairly accurate.

In one recent survey, some of the stellar performances of our most educated youth include the answers to the following question: What major battle was the turning point of the war that led to our nation's independence? The correct answer, Yorktown, was supplied by a very small percentage. The balance either had no idea or guessed it was Gettysburg. In another survey, students were given several maps, one of the United States with state boundaries but without state names. When asked to locate New York, a very high percentage could not. When given a map of the world, a very high percentage could not locate the United States. Most could not locate Iraq, Israel, or Afghanistan, much less the Middle East region. On the bright side, greater than 99% were able to name the current *American Idol* winner. Maybe my priorities need rearranging!

My personal experience has demonstrated to me time and time again the extremely poor mathematical abilities of today's youth (and by the way, our future leadership pool). Go to any local fast food establishment where the majority of employees are retirees, illegal immigrants, or high school kids and you can observe what I have observed. If you go to Wendy's — at least the stores in my area, you will find attached to the cash register an automatic change-dispensing machine. Wendy's is most probably one step ahead of their competitors, at least in regards to cashier shortages, overages, and limiting customer wait time. I am sure that they have learned through experience the necessity of installing these automated change dispensing machines. As it is, it is painful to watch an employee make change for your tendered cash. Even though the electronic cash register displays the amount of change to be returned to the customer, all too often cashiers can be seen to count on their fingers the amount of change to be returned. If someone invented a machine that accepted payment in any form and automatically returned change, I'll bet Wendy's would be the first to place an order to equip every one of its stores with one.

While this is in and of itself painful to watch, it gets worse. In an establishment not equipped with an automatic change-dispensing machine, the cashiers are even more challenged and perplexed because they now need to count out the coin change as well. This usually requires additional time and digits, such as toes. Say your bill comes to $3.05 and you tender $5.05 to the cashier, adding the extra five cents as an afterthought (which I did recently) and after the cashier has already entered your tendered amount of $5. This usually results in instant paralysis, and in a fair amount of cases, total and complete meltdown.

Another lost skill is the ability of cashiers to verbally add your change back to the total bill to equal the amount tendered. I now have come to expect both coins and bills to be lumped together and handed back to me without an accounting. Welcome to the electronic age. If this weren't so serious a topic, it would be easy to laugh it off as pure insanity. Let's step back and think about this for a minute. Every year when surveys are released compiling the results of world rankings depicting where each nation's youth scored on standard tests, the United States consistently falls further and further down the list. Per capita, we as a nation spend the most to educate each child annually, have the best infrastructure money can buy, and with each succeeding year pour more and more money into education than any other nation.

Every other developing nation with which we have to compete on a global basis is pouring out more scientists, engineers, and doctors than we do each year. What is even worse is that so many of the graduates from these foreign countries come here to the United States to obtain college and advanced degrees. Many return home to find employment, participate in strengthening their own country's education system, and end up directly competing against the United States in the global economy! Not only are they eating our lunch, but we are more than willing to serve it to them. If this cycle continues, the bulk of our graduates will actually be serving them lunch, from behind a fast food counter which was probably owned, designed, and built by these foreign graduates. They will also inwardly smile to themselves as the cashier struggles and eventually hands over the change. I am sounding an alarm that we in the United States are in deep trouble! Our educational system, despite being the most expensive one in the world, is failing our children and us miserably, and we better do something about it quickly.

Another major problem is brewing within our higher education system. It seems to me that in the last few years, the graduating class of high school seniors has had a very difficult time with college acceptance. A very high percentage of seniors are being rejected by their top preferences. At first, I attributed this to failure on the part of the students to achieve appropriate scores and sufficient grade levels to qualify for their top choices. This may not necessarily be the case, as more and more I have become aware of many top-notch students who achieve a perfect score on the SATs and graduate valedictorian of their class. Many of these kids are lucky to be accepted by a so-called second tier school.

When my daughter was visiting schools prior to applying, I became aware of a new catchphrase being used by prospective colleges and universities. There is a new emphasis placed upon cultural diversity to round out a student's experience at institutions of higher learning. While touring campuses, I also noticed a tremendous (and what I would consider disproportionate) number of foreign-born students. I recently read somewhere that the reason that we accept so many foreign-born students is the lack of interest on the part of U.S. students in pursuing a degree in the sciences or engineering, and the foreign-born students fill that void. This just doesn't seem right to me, that foreign students occupy so many seats in our institutions of higher education while our own citizens are scrambling to get a seat anywhere.

I do understand the institutions' intent to provide cultural diversity to enhance the education experience, but I also wonder if this is just a charade to justify acceptance of foreign-born students with better grades or the ability to pay full tuition. If the institutions are private, then they certainly have a right to accept whomever they desire. If they are publicly supported in any way, whether it be by federal, state, or local subsidy, in the form of tax exemptions, public grants for research, or taxpayer funding of any sort, including assistance to students, then I would suggest that 95% of all seats be reserved for United States citizens based on academic ability.

In the case of truly private institutions, then I would suggest that a surcharge equal to some amount, say half the annual tuition, be charged all foreign-born (non-U.S. citizens) students with the proceeds being used by the individual states to fund domestic student aid programs. The rational for this surcharge is simply a contributory offset for providing public services while a student is in this country, much in the same way citizens pay state and local taxes for public services.

As a parent of a college student, I personally can attest to the sky-rocketing cost of education. Due to my financial status, I was considered too well off to qualify for any grants; therefore I am too rich to be poor and too poor to afford to pay tuition without putting me or my daughter into serious debt. However, I am bombarded with offers for low cost student loans. These loans have terrific features (NOT) such as deferred start of repayment until six months after the student graduates. And because my credit rating was so good, I would qualify for a super low rate of between 7% and 8%! This was truly a crime. I can get a 30-year fixed rate mortgage for a better rate. If I can barely afford to pay this amount, how in hell is a recently minted student expected to handle this?

Since the cost of higher education has spiraled out of reach of the average family in recent years, this is a problem that needs immediate attention. As part of the recently passed healthcare legislation, a bill was tacked onto this legislation at the last minute which gave the government the monopoly of the student loan market. While this eliminates the banks from lending at such predatory rates, it creates a whole new set of problems. If this legislation makes it easier for students to secure financing, then I fear that institutions of higher learning will find it easier to raise already exorbitant tuition without justification. The government will just open the spigot ever wider. If the colleges and universities were required to find jobs for their graduates, or pay off the student loans, we might find a whole new paradigm shift.

I have some ideas. These ideas may take some time to work through the system, but we must start to implement them immediately. Let's start by examining costs at the elementary and high school levels. In my district, a published figure of the average cost to educate a student per year is somewhere around $14,000. A breakdown of the budget shows that almost 80% of the cost is attributed to staff wages, benefits, and infrastructure (mostly wages and benefits). OK, so we know that everyone needs to be paid for his or her work. I am certainly not opposed to a fair wage for a fair day's work. If all (or let's say 90%) of the student body were attaining levels of achievement commensurate with those of the students from the countries with the best levels of achievement, then there would be less to complain about.

Sorrowfully, our students rank so far down the list that it is actually disgraceful. If you were to put a cost per attainment to each student worldwide, the United States would probably cost 10,000 times as much to educate than that of our more effective competitor countries. However, when I actually analyze the components of the education cost, I quickly zero in on the wage, benefit, and incentive structure of our teachers and administrators.

I can personally attest to many instances where the teacher is licensed and degree-qualified to teach, but simply is not up to par with communication or subject knowledge abilities or, even worse, is just plain lazy, unprepared, or unmotivated. When complaints are registered with the local school board, a typical response is that the teacher has been observed in the classroom on a scheduled basis by the administration and performs within the guidelines set forth to meet standards. If the teacher is tenured, he or she is off limits to corrective actions. Then, he is totally protected by a combination of the administration and the Teachers Union. Once a teacher achieves tenure, he has a job for life unless he commits an offence grievous enough to merit discipline. I will state that this does not apply across the board to all teachers, as many are extremely dedicated and top notch at what they do. What I am really upset about are instances when a system protects those whose performance is sub par, and there are far and away too many cases to be ignored.

Each successive year in elementary education is a building block for future years. In construction, when a foundation block or weight-bearing component is defective, it can and often does lead to structural failure down the line. The same is true for education. If the basic building blocks for science and math are not taught well, there is a greater risk of a student's failure to pursue these fields of study later due to his inability to comprehend course material and his lack of self-confidence in the subject matter. This is cause for real concern, as we as a nation are totally dependent upon our children to secure their own futures as well as ours. Their future success is rooted at the elementary level.

To ensure the greatest magnitude of success, we need to strengthen the curriculum, audit the progress through annual standard testing, and intervene immediately when the results are not satisfactory. The curriculum must have at its core minimum math, science, reading, writing, history, and geography. Basic economics, money and banking, government structure, and current events must be interwoven into the daily curriculum. All these concepts absolutely must be covered daily at the most elementary levels. As students progress through the middle school levels, concepts of chemistry, physics, and advanced technology need to be incorporated. Without these elements, our children will never be able to compete in the domestic economy, much less the global economy.

In fairness to the children, some standards need to be applied to the teachers. All teachers must be qualified to teach their curricula. Teachers must requalify in their curricula at least every two years via a national standards test. Failure to attain a satisfactory level of achievement should result in immediate removal from the classroom — without pay. A teacher can be reinstated upon satisfactory requalification. A teacher's success can in part be quantified by the distribution of scores attained by the students on an annual standard test to be given at the end of each school year. During the year, tests should be administered at logical learning points to ascertain the knowledge level of each student. For those students who do not demonstrate the necessary proficiency, immediate intervention for remediation must occur.

In all fairness to the teachers, it must be recognized that not all students possess the ability or aptitude to excel in all subjects. At the elementary and middle school level, however, all the basic subject matter must be taught and proficiency attained unless there is a demonstrated and diagnosed learning disability that precludes a student from attaining that proficiency. Once a child reaches the high school level, elective classes can be offered according to a child's aptitude. Not all children are destined to become rocket scientists, but all children must be equipped with the fundamental knowledge and ability to function successfully in life on whatever future path they choose. Also in fairness to the teachers, it should be recognized that success on the part of the child in the classroom is greatly dependent upon support in the home. It is not fair to children, teachers, or taxpayers if there is little or no home support. A child needs guidance and structure, such as dedicated time to do homework, and the parent or guardian has the responsibility to ensure homework is completed.

While the United States mandates that all children be provided with a public school education, it is the taxpayers who support this with their taxes, and their hard-earned monies should not be squandered.

Children who are unprepared should not be allowed in the classroom, as this only serves to disrupt and slow down the learning process for everyone else. Strict academic standards should be imposed both at the individual student and overall school level. Any student falling below a prescribed academic standard (such as uniform test scores) should be prohibited from participation in any extracurricular activity, be it school clubs or sports teams, until the prescribed academic standard is maintained for an additional year after falling below standard. Schools that fall below standard should be mandated to replace extracurricular activities with remedial classes focusing on the areas of deficiency.

If need be, an alternative solution may be to designate a regional learning center to enroll deficient students who would be given very focused help, depending upon the volume of students requiring such services. This would preclude the need to penalize schools and students who would meet standards but for a few low performing students. The incentive for those attending regional centers would be to improve to a point where they could return to a school offering the full spectrum of extracurricular activities. Remember, these are just some preliminary ideas and the correct, effective solution needs to be designed via a collaborative effort of school district, taxpayers, and academics.

Charter schools, a relatively new idea where everyone, parents, students, and teachers all have skin in the game, are another concept that if proven successful is a very good alternative.

The world of academia, at least at the local level, should be made to conform to and mimic the business environment. The citizens who support the academic environment and who are employers or employees themselves know the harsh realities of the competitive business world well. When economic times are difficult, employers must face reality to survive. To maintain a functioning and profitable business providing employment opportunities, sometimes costs are the overriding survival factor. Benefits and wages are always subject to change, depending upon the fiscal year's bottom line. In good years, both or one or the other may rise; in bad years, both or one or the other may remain static or decrease. Additionally, the individual employee's performance becomes a determining factor in all cases. When a company is profitable and employees perform well, they are usually rewarded for outstanding efforts. When an employee is judged to be a poor performer, he is either fired or, if very lucky, put on probation for a period of time and given the opportunity to improve performance. There is no guarantee of future employment or salary increase for anyone, let alone poor performers.

These same standards should apply to our school systems. Tenure should be done away with completely. Year after year, I have seen contract talks with the teachers union result in basically the same outcome. It seems that the union always ends up with a negotiated annual salary increase that is always way above that of industry. Benefits for teachers are noncontributory, time off is extremely generous, and guaranteed increases are given for attaining additional credit hours. The wage and benefit structure of teaching professionals in my school district defies logic and sucks the lifeblood out of the community via school taxes. Wages and benefits should be based partly on private industry standards and partly on what the community can reasonably afford. I would suggest that wages be indexed to the average gross income of a community in which the school is located. Benefits should be contributory, the same as industry, and instead of a noncontributory pension, a 401(k) type of plan should be instituted. The annual school budget should be developed to include a match, dollar for dollar, up to the first 6% of voluntary contributions. When everyone else in the working community must fund his own retirement, where there is no guarantee of return, there is no reason why teaching professionals should not do likewise. School budget votes should also be modified to reflect the wishes of the community. As they are today, a district budget approval can be accomplished simply by having one vote more for as opposed to against.

First of all, I believe that only those who pay school taxes should be allowed to vote on the budget. Secondly, I believe that a 75% majority should be required for passage. School administrators must demonstrate fiscal responsibility regarding the proposed budget. If they are going to be paid like CEOs, then they must be accountable like CEOs. Education has become an extremely expensive proposition, and there are limits on how much of a burden can be placed upon a community to support it, before the community chest runs dry.

Teachers and administrators must be held to the same standards as those who pay their taxes to support the school system they belong to. Teachers whose students collectively attain high scores on standard tests should be rewarded accordingly. Conversely, those judged ineffective should be put on probation and given the opportunity to improve their performance. Those who fail to improve should be let go. Teaching is a very demanding, noble profession the importance of which should not be underestimated. Our children's futures are in the hands of teachers. Teachers who have proven themselves proficient should be rewarded accordingly.

As I have touched on before, the dearth of homegrown science and math majors in this country will eventually lead this country to ruin if it is not reversed. We have already witnessed the massive decline in manufacturing jobs due to the creation of less costly labor markets offshore. What we are left with is an overabundance of unskilled low wage service industry jobs. These types of jobs will not ensure a secure high standard of living for the workforce of the future.

There was a time not too long ago when the entire world looked to this country for the technological advances that would power the world for the future. The scientists and engineers who graduated from our universities were responsible for developing technologies that were designed into products manufactured in this country and exported worldwide. This was the formula for high-paying skilled jobs, a trade surplus as opposed to a trade deficit, national security powered by technology, secure retirement years with guaranteed pensions, and an ever-increasing standard of living. Those times, I'm afraid, no longer exist.

We depend upon imports for most of the products we purchase, and those imports are designed and manufactured by foreign countries. Our high skilled jobs that once paid good salaries from which were generated sufficient taxes to support our government spending and high standard of living, are now in other countries. Instead, we continually run up massive foreign trade deficits annually, along with unheard of massive Federal budget deficits. Sooner rather than later, this country will become bankrupt both monetarily and intellectually. We will owe so much money in the form of U.S. Government securities to foreign countries, that our currency will lose its value, and foreigners will no longer want to accept our government securities or dollars in return for purchases. Then, my friends, we will cease to be of any consequence to anybody. We cannot let this happen. There is still time to reverse course and reestablish America's preeminent place in the world community, but we must embark on the necessary changes now.

I propose an idea to mitigate this situation and it is directly tied to industry, social security, Medicare, and education. Each segment provides a structural component integral to the support and success of the idea. Let's start with linking in an idea for funding Social Security. By allowing the Social Security fund to invest directly into American-based companies, thereby strengthening their balance sheets and additionally providing lower-cost liquidity, we as a nation can also benefit from these companies.

Companies in every sector of industry must continually recruit and compete for talented personnel to stay competitive. As is often the case, this recruitment occurs on college campuses, and via search firms. It is not unusual for companies to end up hiring foreign nationals either from schools or from abroad due to a dearth of technological talent. Oftentimes, the search results in a less than perfect fit due to a mismatch in skill set.

The shortfall of U.S. citizens graduating with degrees in science, engineering, technology, or math is disheartening. These high-paying jobs are going to people who in many cases are not citizens. I would propose that these American companies band together to create institutions of higher learning for the sole purpose of acting as an incubator and source of future talent from which to recruit. These institutions, whose underlying indirect funding would be derived from government program investment, could be reserved for U.S. citizens. The curricula could be designed to fit the requirements of U.S. business, since they are ultimately the potentially future employers of graduates of these institutions.

What has traditionally been the hallmark of the United States is the technological leadership in design, and the ability to bring to market the products developed in the laboratories and drawing boards of U.S. companies. Without the pool of highly educated and qualified students to feed our companies, the future prospects for U.S. economic leadership will diminish rapidly.

The underlying indirect funding derived from government program investment works this way. Social Security payments to the government, either in whole or in part, could be allocated to private accounts that in turn are invested in U.S. companies via stock purchases. For a company to qualify to be on the stock purchase list, a number of requirements would be in order. First, the company must be U.S.-based. Second, a prescribed percentage of its employees worldwide must be U.S. citizens. Third, the company must participate in the U.S. higher education program, meaning that some of the revenue derived from Social Security–based stock purchases must be allocated to support U.S. institutions of higher learning. Fourth, graduates of these institutions must be given first consideration for employment within these companies. Fifth, corporate compensation structures of these companies must be relative to reality, from the CEO to the factory-floor worker. A factory-floor worker's wage in effect is subsidized by the lower, in-line management wage.

My point here is two-fold. The U.S. government should never be a party to paying outrageous salaries or compensation to management of a company benefiting from this initiative. Second, nonmanagement employees must also derive some benefit, that being in the form of higher compensation. This should easily be accomplished by stock grants, better benefit structures, and higher hourly wages. Even a tiny slice of what overly compensated CEOs are paid will subsidize this.

Organized labor should not look upon this initiative as a free pass to raid the cookie jar. If organized labor has a base in the companies taking part, then they (organized labor) must conform to mandatory third-party arbitration if an impasse of labor negotiations occurs. If labor costs and rules become excessive, then the company will fail and the whole concept collapses like a house of cards. Everybody loses! For this initiative to work, all must be responsible. This initiative is designed to build wealth for all involved and to benefit all.

Chapter 11

Social Security

Franklin Roosevelt, a Democrat, introduced the Social Security (FICA) Program. He promised that participation in the program would be completely voluntary.

As with anything else in society, if there is an absolute need for a law, program, or policy, it usually requires a mandate by the government to be implemented. If there weren't any undue outside influences from political parties, PACs, campaign contributors, etc., our elected officials could most likely be trusted to get it right most of the time. Absent these ingredients, there might be an outbreak of common sense, and the will of the people would prevail. However, when reality rears its ugly head, we inevitably end up with something that solves or resolves the original problem only directly proportional to the extent of "pork" tacked onto the legislative bill. I like to think of this as greasing the wheels of government. After all, our elected representatives need to show their constituents, campaign contributors, and PACs that they are adept at bringing home the bacon and protecting/promoting the interests of those generous supporters who got them elected in the first place.

The system works very well for everyone except the constituents who get the bacon. Their arteries fill with grease and they die of a heart attack when it comes time to pay the tax bill. If you think of this process as going out to a diner for lunch, the law, program, or policy is the entrée and the pork is the tip for service, albeit a very generous tip.

There is no free lunch. This is insane! Should the passage of a law, program, or policy be dependent upon the funding of a bridge to nowhere in Alaska, a study of the mating habits of the Texas armadillo, or the color preference of ketchup for Pennsylvanians? I think not. It should be based solely on its own merits without any undue outside influence. This pork is killing us. If we were to eliminate the pork, or as it is now referred to, "earmarks" (which, by the way, are seldom discussed in detail by the politicians who requested or are the beneficiaries of them), we would probably have enough money in the federal budget to properly fund all the essential government social programs mandated by law.

One of the most important of these essential government social programs is Social Security. Social Security also happens to be a default pension for far too many Americans. This program was designed to be a supplement to other retirement benefits accrued over the course of one's working career, not one's sole retirement benefits. The fund is running out of money, although no one knows exactly when it will happen. That all depends upon who is talking, on what day, and what party the speaker represents. I also confess to not knowing exactly how the Social Security Trust Fund works, how much is left, how much has been borrowed against it for non-Social Security reasons, when the money will run out, or all of its basis of funding. I know that payroll deductions fund a major part, and I think interest on U.S. securities that were issued when the federal government borrows from the fund are also part of the funding stream. In any event, this program is a sacred cow for all Americans, especially for those nearing or in retirement.

Politicians know this all too well. If there is one hot button issue that can be used to incite emotions or as a scare tactic, just talk about changing or fiddling with Social Security. You will be guaranteed to give a multitude of senior citizens a heart attack, because they depend too much on the program for their financial existence, and talk of change will push them over the edge. That is why this topic, Social Security, is called the "third rail of politics." It is also why Bush's proposal to allow individuals to control a tiny percent of their allocation via alternative investments was defeated. I thought the proposal was theoretically a good one, but it just didn't go far enough. All too quickly it became a political football, and if passed would reflect better on one party than the other. That, my friends, is called partisan politics, of the elected officials, by the elected officials, and for the elected officials and let the citizens be dammed! Our wise elected officials saw fit to scare the crap out of everyone with doomsday predictions of fraud, incompetence on the part of the individual to manage their 2% slice, greedy brokerage firms overcharging and getting fat on trading commissions, and total collapse of the fund. Truth be told, this is an issue that should rise above politics, as should all issues, but our lamebrain politicians just don't get it.

Let's take a different approach, sort of think outside of the box. We know that the current crop of baby boomers has already begun to retire and tons more will retire and draw upon Social Security over the next twenty or more years. The number of working people needed to support this gigantic withdrawal is probably two to three times what exists. Simple math or deduction tells us that the fund cannot support this payout without drastically raising the retirement age and/or drastically increasing the Social Security tax. An alternative would be to borrow to support the fund. None of these options is desirable, palatable, or fiscally responsible — it would just be status quo, bury our head in the sand, and hope everything works out. I suspect that just investing the fund's funds in 12-month CDs would be a better approach, at least earning a 5% return. This would not solve the problem anyway. Here is my suggestion to forever solve the funding problem.

Historically speaking, I believe the stock market has returned on average about 15% a year. Since I have awoken and realized that I am closer to retirement than I'd like to admit, I also realized that I needed to pay close attention to the 401(k) and other IRAs to which I have been contributing over the years. I cannot depend upon our elected officials to fix Social Security in time for me to retire, and anyway I couldn't depend upon Social Security to provide for me in my retirement unless I drastically lowered my standard of living. I am sorry to say that this is currently the case for all too many retirees. Even if COLAs and all the senior tax discounts are applied to local taxes, I know that most seniors' Social Security payments are totally eaten up by irresponsibly raised school taxes and healthcare costs. Their dreams of living out their sunset years in comfort evaporate as quickly as a drop of water on a hot, sunny, dry day. Not only that, but for future retirees to maximize the monthly payout, they will need to continue to work until they are 66 or 72 years of age, forgoing an earlier retirement for a bigger monthly check. This is not only sad, it is WRONG!!!

Since I've begun to manage my own retirement funds, I have found that I can achieve a fairly high annual return by just doing a little bit of homework and paying attention to the worlds of business, history, and politics. I am not bragging, I am just stating fact. You may at this point be very tempted to debate this statement in light of the recent downturn in the market. Yes, you have a perfect right to be skeptical, but, as I stated, the market returns on the average 15% a year over the long run. I invest in mutual funds. I also invest in individual equities, and I also lose my shirt there. I do not have the expertise or the time to be a successful investor in individual stocks. Mutual funds however are a completely different story. If I can achieve such good returns, there is no reason why the Social Security fund can't be managed to the same standards.

I like to stay on top of the business world, and hence spend a lot of time listening to Bloomberg radio, reading the World Street Journal, and watching cable business channels. There is no dearth of qualified experts in the financial community whose talents could be employed to make an expertly managed Social Security fund happen. In all media, there is a constant parade of fund managers, stock pickers, and economists who are talented enough to make short work of righting the Social Security ship. Jim Jubak, Lawrence Kudlow, Jim "Mad Money" Cramer, or even Warren Buffet might be enticed to take up this challenge. These names are only a few examples of the illustrious market superstars who could be tapped.

Yeah, I can hear you now...Wall Street in bed with the federal government! Before you go running off into the night screaming collusion, hear me out. Most people, that includes our esteemed elected officials, are either terrified of or don't trust Wall Street. There is a legitimate reason for this when it comes to corruption and less than honest business dealings. When it comes down to business, there is no great mystique, once you comprehend economics, accounting, and business. It's really quite straightforward. How could this possibly work you ask?

First of all, and I freely admit that I do not know the current status of the Social Security fund. It would have to be determined if there are monies available to invest. Though there may be some leeway, more than likely we are existing hand to mouth, just ahead of the piper, paying out checks from the input stream with little or no reserve. If this were the case, then we as a country need to make a commitment to borrow enough, yes, by increasing the deficit or by reducing other spending, to fund Social Security payouts for 13 or 14 months. The theory here is that the cost of borrowing would be more than offset by the return generated by market returns. Historically speaking, this should hold true.

It may take a few years to build up enough profit to repay the borrowed funds, but eventually the fund would become cash-flow positive, and even further down the road might become, should I dare to say, self-sufficient. These funds would be invested in actual or quasi-mutual funds. Our panel of market experts could determine the makeup of these funds. The funds could be a variety of existing funds or funds newly created for this purpose. Fund managers would buy and sell through their affiliated brokerages that in turn would execute trades for their customary, or government negotiated discount fees. But, before this relationship could work, a number of rules must be set down.

First, these holdings would be held in a blind trust, with only the expert panel knowledgeable of its composition and trade executions. The Securities and Exchange Commission in conjunction with the Treasury Department would oversee this. Second, all management fees would be forfeited if the fund on an annual basis did not achieve its previously agreed-upon stated returns after fees are subtracted. This puts the experts' money where their mouths are. Third, these funds could be invested only in United States of America companies. This in effect would be an indirect reinvestment in America, which might piss off other governments or violate some arcane World Trade Organization rules, but would in fact be similar to the support given to many European and Chinese companies by their respective governments. A fourth regulation would be that all employed individuals of working age must contribute to a 401(k) on a weekly basis to participate in Social Security.

As a country, we probably have the lowest savings rate in the free world. A mandatory deduction of even 1% or 2% on a weekly basis over the course of a working career would hardly impact an individual's take-home pay and would compound to a meaningful amount by the time that person is ready for retirement. We have to remember that corporate pensions are going the way of the dinosaur, and retirement investments must be portable. Most importantly, we must remember that Social Security was intended to be a supplement to retirement funds, not the sole retirement fund.

If this new Social Security strategy were set up, I could envision a future where Americans could possibly retire at an earlier age, receiving monthly Social Security checks in relatively equal or actually larger payouts than are currently scheduled. Additionally and optimistically, as the fund grows over the years, I would suggest some of my own earmarks for this legislation. Two immediate goals would be to fund a healthcare trust with seed money to act as an annuity for the support of Medicare and, secondly, to do the same for an education trust.

This is a relatively simple solution to a potentially expensive future implosion of the Social Security system. Just think about this for a minute. The politicians will scream bloody murder because they cannot possibly agree to something that is good for the country without getting a piece of the action for themselves. Even if they comprehended the architecture and benefits, they would subject any proposal of this sort to analysis paralysis for years until all our elected officials figured out a way to claim kudos for such a program. I guarantee that the financial wizards of Wall Street could put this together in no time flat with such good results that if it were a publicly traded fund, Morningstar would give it a six-star rating!

There are also many indirect benefits that would accrue from such a program. By investing in American Business, we would lower the cost of capital for these companies, leading to expansion, more employment, and more tax revenues, ultimately raising the standard of living for the American populace. If I sat down and actually thought about the ripple effect, I could probably go on and on with benefits, but I would rather leave that to someone like Lawrence Kudlow and expert panels to dissect, as their findings would be more comprehensive and accurate.

Chapter 12

National Security

"History teaches that war begins when governments believe the price of aggression is cheap."

—Ronald Reagan

S ome might say that death in the service of one's country is a noble act, and while it may be so, death is also indiscriminate, colorblind, and tragic. Let our opponents, whoever they may be, revel in the glory of death to their own, while we rejoice in the avoidance of casualties to our own. Nothing short of a very strong, modernized, well-prepared, and well-equipped military will help us achieve that goal if war is inevitable.

Let's start this topic with a little background on me. During most of the Vietnam War, I was a high school student. While I was in college, the military draft lottery was instituted and my birthday was picked somewhere in the middle of the pack. Luckily for me and most others who were eligible, the war ended with the Paris Peace Accords, before I could be called up. At that time in my life, early in high school, I was pretty politically naïve and really never researched the history of Vietnam, or just why and how we became entangled in that conflict. During my early years of college, I began to pay much more attention to the hows and whys of Vietnam. I still didn't fully comprehend the politics that landed us there, other than we were fighting the spread of Communism. What I did understand, though, was that getting drafted and sent to Vietnam was not at all high on anyone's list of things to do, as there was a high probability of returning with a purple heart or not returning at all.

No matter, if I was called, I was not going to run away to Canada. I believed in our government, understood that military service might be the price I had to pay, and felt that because I was a citizen of this country, it was my patriotic duty. The nightly news was filled with coverage of the war, protests against the war, and something that I never really noticed before, truly heated and passionate politics revolving around the war. The battlefield footage broadcast, and the photographs in newspapers and magazines, although somewhat sensitized, were not something that could be ignored — they were horrific. The antiwar protesters and the counterculture that was born as a result of Vietnam didn't really sit well with me. Initially, I thought that campus unrest, protests, and antiwar rallies, while disturbing to me because they tore at the fabric of my country, were a perfectly acceptable way for the public to voice its opposition to the war. But, I came to believe the resulting counterculture of hippies with their free love, drugs, and protest music made a sideshow of what serious opposition was trying to bring about.

Vietnam was a monumental loss for this country. Idealistically speaking, it was probably the right thing to do, as its goals from a foreign policy standpoint could have been conceived as admirable. However, supporting a morally bankrupt and corrupt puppet South Vietnamese government put us behind the eight ball before we even started, and the price we paid was far too excessive for any benefits derived. We should have learned a military lesson from Vietnam, because history is bound to repeat itself, and indeed it has in Lebanon, Somalia, Iraq, and now Afghanistan. Regardless of the politics that get us into these conflicts/wars, we'd better be sure that when we commit to put boots on the ground we do it in the same way, with the same commitment, and with the same result that was demonstrated by World

War I, World War II, and Desert Storm. Anything less is a betrayal to us all.

Since 9/11 the geopolitics of the world have changed dramatically and so has the composition and abilities of our enemies. Post World War II and pre 9/11, the United States was involved in several conflicts. The Korean War, the Vietnam War, and Desert Storm were military conflicts that involved major commitments of men, materials, and combat. Casualties, KIA, MIA, and wounded were substantial in Korea and Vietnam. With the exception of modern fighter-jet aircraft and the introduction of helicopters, Korea was a war fought with outdated equipment left over from World War II. Although this was conventional warfare, we were ill-prepared and incapable of conducting military operations in a manner that would limit battlefield casualties.

During Vietnam, state of the art (for that time period) jet aircraft along with tactical aircraft were employed with good results. Helicopters played a prominent role in the transportation of men and materials in medivac operations, while gunships provided offensive firepower. The M16 rifle became standard issue and, despite its many drawbacks, was a marked improvement over past equipment issue. If Vietnam had been a conventional type of war, we would have fared far better than we actually did. Vietnam was anything but conventional, and once again we paid a very high price in blood and treasure for our ill-preparedness. We did learn many lessons, and our KIA count was substantially lower than what might have been. Major advances in medical evacuation and near front-line treatment saved the lives of many men who in earlier wars would have otherwise died before they could be treated.

Nestled between the Vietnam War and Desert Storm was another war that did not involve combat operations, the Cold War. This war actually began before the end of World War II and encompassed both

Korea and Vietnam, but ended before Desert Storm. It was during the time period between the end of the Vietnam War and Desert Storm that our military experienced major implementations of both tactics and equipment. Though no actual combat operations occurred during this war, the ever-present threat of hostilities with the Soviet Union dictated the need for extensive training, maneuvers, and technologically driven equipment upgrades, resulting in a military that was much better prepared to engage in combat operations. This became clearly evident before, during, and after the Desert Storm operation in Kuwait and Iraq. The one commonality that all these wars had (with the partial exception of Vietnam) was the existence of an enemy that was recognizable. Post 9/11, during the War on Terror, we are faced with an enemy of different stripes that presents us with a whole new set of rules and challenges.

National security is no longer confined to just massive military might. With the advances in internet technology, our military and civilian operations have become extremely dependent upon telecommunications for everyday fulfillment of our needs. On 9/11, when the World Trade Center towers were attacked, we saw just how vulnerable and dependent we were on telecommunications. When the towers collapsed, cell phone coverage was severely disrupted. This was the first real unplanned test of our telecom infrastructure and the resulting loss of service clearly exhibited our vulnerability. Our telecom infrastructure needs to be expanded with triple and even quadruple redundancy with backup-secure, shielded landlines to survive similar threats in the future.

Recently, we have also witnessed attacks on the internet through viruses and overloaded servers, resulting in severe slowdowns and even loss of service for extended periods of time. Another instance recently reported was the deliberate cyber attack on the Pentagon telecommunications. These are becoming more frequent. If these were to become successful, our military could be put at extreme risk of performing any military actions. Satellite-based telecommunications are also at risk. These attacks have not been officially blamed upon anyone, but I believe that we suspect the Chinese military and government. While I am far from being an expert in these areas, common sense tells me we need to beef up our security and provide for redundant systems to counter any threats.

Along these same lines, one of our major (primary) military telecommunications vendors (3com) was pursued for purchase by a Chinese businessman. Upon further investigation, it was determined that this person was a former high-ranking official in the Chinese Army. When suspicion was raised and after the results of the investigation were revealed, the deal was taken off the table. Due to instances of this nature, where public companies are contractors of military equipment, I believe that changes for the sake of national security need to be made. Whenever a company is designing, manufacturing, or in any way involved with sensitive military equipment, there needs to be some sort of partition or barrier within the company that prevents and isolates that portion from the balance of the company. We cannot ever afford to have our secrets compromised by any means, especially by something as simple as just buying a company.

The military is our first and foremost "long" arm of protection. It is not the only arm, but it is the arm that most nations are well aware of and respect without qualification. The infrastructure upon which our military is based is of utmost importance. The equipment upon which our armed forces rely will usually greatly determine the outcome of any conflict in which they are involved.

There have been disturbing developments involving our procurement of military equipment that everyone should be aware of and concerned about. Our military recently bid to replace our aging air tanker fleet. A foreign government-sponsored company EADS (European Aeronautical Defense Systems), the makers of Airbus airplanes in partnership with Northrup Co., successfully bid on this contract and beat out Boeing Aircraft. While in this case, the governments sponsoring EADS are our allies, I do not feel that this is a good practice. Over time, any of these governments may no longer be allies of ours, and a foreign adversary having design and manufacture details of our military systems is outright foolish. When it comes to military equipment, I believe that only American companies should be allowed to supply American military equipment.

Also, due to the nature of our global economy, many electronic components in our weapons systems are of foreign manufacture and/or assembly. This really puts us in a precarious situation. In time of war, our ability to replace needed equipment becomes compromised if the component manufacturers are on the other side.

I suggest that a program be instituted within the military industrial complex of this country in which all weapons systems, electronic components, and materials of any kind essential to support the military in time of conflict be evaluated. The evaluation should include the source of manufacture, an estimation of how critical the component/system is, the availability of its resupply, the lead time for resupply, and its susceptibility to sabotage by its source of manufacture. After the evaluation is complete, any item that fails the criteria set for safe resupply should be put on a fast track for replacement by a supply line of production within the United States.

During World War II, the United States became known as the Arsenal of Democracy because we mobilized our industrial complex to shift rapidly from a consumer goods production base to a military one. While we shifted quickly, it required enormous planning and expense to accomplish the switch to start producing and then filling the pipeline with military equipment. The technologies of that time were not nearly as advanced as those of today, and our weapons were much simpler to produce. If we were to become engaged in a protracted period of hostilities, I would have serious doubts as to whether our ability to sustain our resupply effort would be effective, especially if our sources of supply were compromised. If for no other reason than to keep our resupply ability on a footing of wartime readiness, we should keep all lines of production up and running even if it is on a very limited basis. This would ensure that if the need to expand suddenly occurred, we could do so with little or no delay. The last thing our military needs is to be on the battlefield without equipment because the necessary components to operate the weapons systems are not available.

Another benefit to this switch is our ability to constantly introduce upgrades to existing equipment until a wholesale replacement with next generation equipment is in place. There were also countless instances during past hostilities where the most advanced systems could not satisfy our needs, but simpler (last generation) weapons systems were more appropriate. The ability to reintroduce mass production of such systems should be designed into our procurement systems.

I believe that in many ways the current war in Iraq has been an eye opener, both for the military and for the citizens of the United States. This country has, in recent times, relied upon the projection of tremendous force and firepower to quell our adversaries' appetite to wage war with us. Desert Storm demonstrated the capabilities of the United States military to the world. After 9/11, we demonstrated the same capabilities in Afghanistan and Iraq. Regardless of one's opinions toward the necessity of engaging in war with these countries, the fact remains that we did. Our initial successes were no less impressive than what was experienced during Desert Storm. But those initial successes proved to be just that — initial!

Once the Taliban and Al Qaeda forces in Afghanistan were deposed of, we turned our sights on Iraq and paid insufficient attention to Afghanistan. Our military was diverted to Iraq where we achieved the same initial successes. What was not taken into consideration was the duration of the effort necessary to bring the wars to a satisfactory end. In Afghanistan, the enemy melted away and returned to fight a war using guerilla tactics. In Iraq, the populace that was expected to welcome the victors (that being us) with open arms did not. Instead, we became immersed in a civil war scenario for which we were totally unprepared.

When the Vietnam War came to a conclusion, the populace of this country was both weary and distrustful of the military. The immediate need for manpower was lessened, the extremely unpopular military draft ended, and eventually we filled our military ranks with a volunteer army. While we were still in the throes of a Cold War with the Soviet Union, our troops were no longer engaged in active combat. Our military embarked upon a new strategy using tremendous advances in technology, which in turn lessened the need for as many boots on the ground as had been previously necessary. Intensive training and deployment of new advanced weapons systems garnered the respect of our adversaries and kept them at bay. The concept of a volunteer army proved successful as the numbers and quality of enlistments, supplemented by reserves and National Guard, filled the military's manpower requirements. Our global concentrations of military forces were mostly deployed in Japan, Korea, and Europe, mainly Germany. When President Reagan raised the stakes by increasing the military budget for development of a Star Wars space based defense system, the Soviet Union threw in the towel. Their economy, already a shambles, could not support the necessary escalation in military spending necessary to support countermeasures for Reagan's new systems.

The Soviet Union basically imploded, the Berlin Wall came down, Communism disappeared with a shift to capitalism and Glasnost, and a sort of peace took hold. Reagan's military budget was cut and the U.S Congress couldn't wait to get its hands on the "Peace Dividend." The military underwent many rounds of budget cuts, resulting in force reductions, base closings, and mothballing/scrapping/decommissioning of equipment/vessels/weapons systems. The military allocated its budget carefully, investing in technological advances to weapons systems and replacement of aging equipment with more advanced high-ticket items, though they were fewer in number. The shift toward technology over manpower had taken place. The ensuing time period between Vietnam and Desert Storm required little in the way of military force projection, and the necessary resources available were more than adequate to handle needs.

When Saddam Hussein decided to reclaim his lost province (Kuwait) via military conquest, he bit off more than he could chew. Kuwait and his next victim in line, Saudi Arabia, were unwilling dance partners. If he thought for one second that the United States was about to let him control the primary source(s) of our oil imports, he gravely miscalculated. Saddam had built a very sizable and formidable military force for the region. Maybe his hubris got the better of him and maybe he figured that neither the United States nor anyone else would risk a humiliating military defeat on his turf. The world, however, saw things differently. With a little bit of arm-twisting, the United States formed a coalition of countries, sanctioned by the United Nations, to inform Saddam of his miscalculation. Although the coalition was uneasy at best (this was historic, as before this Arab countries would not fight a brother Arab country), a combination of fear, a dose of reality, and the pressure of world opinion were all George H. Bush needed. A battle plan was drawn up and men, supplies, and military equipment were mobilized and staged to Saudi Arabia.

The resulting war was almost over before it started. A combination of excellent planning, tactical movement, and highly effective use of weapons systems technologically far superior to anything Saddam could field resulted in the most lopsided victory ever imagined. This was truly an exhibition of massive force projection. No hostile forces hindered that mobilization of necessary forces and equipment to conduct this war. This was fortunate and played a major role in the conduct of this war.

During World Wars I and II, transport of men and equipment from the United States to the fields of battle was much more of a challenge. Hostile forces were always a serious concern, and many supply ships were lost to enemy action.

This issue was not present in the war in Iraq, yet it still took an inordinate amount of time to logistically position our military for attack. In a sense, we were lucky. I question our ability to do what is required if we are faced with more challenging situations.

The Iraq war has severely tested our ability to wage war with our current military forces. We have had to deploy the regular Army, National Guard units, and Reserve units to meet our military needs. Further, the deployments have been for multiple extended tours in the combat zone. Regardless of what the Pentagon officials might say, I believe that our military forces have been stretched to the limit. Our forces have performed magnificently, but we have asked more of them than we should have. During World War II, tours of duty were for the duration plus. In times of national emergency this is necessary. The Iraq war is not necessarily a time of national emergency. Our Guard and Reserve units have been deployed for time periods for which they were not prepared and did not realistically expect to serve. This has put an unrealistic strain and disruption upon the families left behind to cope with financial and psychological burdens. And this alone seriously undermines the effectiveness of our fighting forces. This responsibility clearly needs to be spread across a much wider segment of the population to be equitable and manageable. The concept of a volunteer army has been proven beyond a shadow of a doubt unequal to the need to fill military ranks with the personnel qualified to successfully conduct prolonged operations on a wartime footing. We have quite literally worn our troops out. We have also quite literally worn out our equipment and stretched our resupply capabilities past the point of reason.

These factors present us with an extremely dangerous and tenuous situation. We have already witnessed our inability to properly "surge" troops to the level needed for the Afghanistan engagement. We are depending on the withdrawal of overworked troops from Iraq to fill these needs. Hypothetically, if we were to become engaged in Iran or anywhere else, I do not believe we could successfully deploy the necessary troop and equipment levels needed. To take the point further, if the deployment were required in a geographically opposite or divergent region of the world where supply was not easily accomplished (like what happened with World War II European and Pacific theaters), our readiness factor would be severely compromised. We would have to either declare a national emergency and mobilize the civilian population, or let the additional threat/hostilities go uncontested, maybe to our detriment. We cannot ever allow ourselves to be put in this position.

My proposed solution to these serious pitfalls will most likely be politically unpopular at best and fiercely contested and derided at worst. All I can say is that drastic times call for drastic measures. I have already addressed the readiness factor of equipment and weapons supply:

it is easy logistically. The hard part is associated with the funding of such a readiness factor. I can only look back to President Ronald Reagan and borrow his example of drastically increasing the military budget. While unpalatable, offsets to the taxes required to fund such a venture would be the increased employment provided by the businesses that are engaged in the supply effort. The benefits of putting people (many currently displaced by the effects of a global economy) back to work receiving salaries and benefits, and paying taxes instead of relying on government programs and subsidies to survive, will partially offset the required funding. The balance will have to come from a balanced federal budget process. As I said, that was the easy part.

The hard part of the solution is the reinstitution of the draft. Many of the ideas that I put forth in this book are not necessarily mine alone. Congressman Charles Rangel of New York proposed reinstituting the draft on many occasions. But his reasons and mine differ. I believe the Congressman wanted to do this because he felt that the weight of the Volunteer Army was falling disproportionately upon the shoulders of the minority communities of this country. I also believe that his reasoning was that joining the military was viewed as a last and desperate act of economic survival for many of the volunteers. Lacking the education and skills needed to compete for higher paying jobs/careers in the civilian sector, many people joined the military as an escape from a less promising life. I believe that both these points are true, but I also believe that the military has provided these individuals with an opportunity to improve their future, and if there hadn't been a military to join, their future would have been much less promising. The notion that the more privileged youth of this country escape military service cannot be discounted. The ranks of the military are disproportionately filled with minorities. The general officer corps is also disproportionately filled with nonminorities. These ranks are more heavily comprised of graduates of the military academies whose entry requirements are usually far out of reach of the minority populations. That is not to say that minorities are not represented within the officer ranks or opportunities for advancement within the military are denied to minorities. Fewer nonminorities than minorities view the military as an enticing career and choose to join. So, yes, the Congressman is correct regarding those issues.

I believe that military service should no longer be an option for citizens of this country, but rather a duty, for two reasons. First, our military needs to be of sufficient size to meet any and all requirements for deployment wherever and whenever necessary. We cannot possibly do this now without a general mobilization of the population. Even if the population were to be mobilized, training the draftees would most likely result in untold and costly delays in deployment. When every minute counts, delays of months are simply unacceptable. Second and equally as important is the simple fact that if every household or a majority of households in this country were to have members in the armed forces, the politicians — our elected officials — would think long and hard before committing our military to a hostile action. As it stands now, an extremely high percentage of elected officials do not have family members serving in the military. It is a lot easier to vote on something that does not have a direct impact on your own family than it is when your own family members could be put at great risk. If we all had skin in the game, I believe that we would be far less likely to be as bold or reckless with our foreign policy as we are today. War is a high stakes proposition and should be respected as such.

When I speak of military service, I am not just thinking of a two-year commitment to the armed forces. I truly believe that in today's environment we must be prepared to act very quickly in time of need. The faster we can react, the less likely that hostilities will be initiated or prolonged, and the less likely that casualties will be incurred. The possibility of engagement with our military forces should provoke enough fear that it becomes a deterrent in and of itself.

Therefore, I would recommend that we model our military service on the system as Israel's. Every able-bodied person from 18 to 40 should be obligated to enter the armed forces for a period of two years. This cadre would become our standing regular army. Two-year tours with periodic refresher training (as the Reserves currently receive) should become the standard. All citizens from 41 to 65 should be designated as support personnel and be required to fill positions of supply, administration, medical support, etc., either domestically or rear area, according to need and skill set in the event of a national emergency. Initial training and periodic refresher orientations should become standard.

By implementing this sort of structure, we would enhance our war readiness and supplement the work handled by the National Guard. This serves many purposes. The National Guard should only function as military combat reserves in times of a national emergency, such as a full-blown war, but they must be kept in a state of readiness for a domestic role. Natural disasters, such as floods, hurricanes, tornados, wildfires, and national priorities such as epidemics and border patrol should be the purview of the National Guard. The National Guard should be a logical extension of FEMA as well.

The regular standing armed forces could still be of a volunteer nature, which offers incentives to career path development for those wishing to pursue a career in the military.

That segment of the population wishing to pursue civilian-based careers, and armed forces retirees who are from 40 to 60, should be given the opportunity to become Armed Forces Reserves. This group would automatically supplement the Regular Standing Armed Forces in time of war or hostilities. Each segment of the Armed Forces — Regular,

Reserves, and National Guard — should be given incentives at appropriate levels of compensation to fill the ranks. Extended tours or reenlistments should be accompanied by increased compensation. Regardless of direction taken, the obligation to serve and to attend refresher training periodically would be mandatory for all.

One of the big lessons we have learned from the Iraq war is the need to support our deployed military personnel emotionally, financially, and medically. Paramount is the need to relieve those serving of the distractions of civilian life at home. If either the Reserves or National Guard are called for deployment, the minimum that the government should do is to help pay the cost of insurance policies (auto home, health), suspend or supplement all debt payments such as credit, mortgage, utility, etc., during their deployment, and guarantee full employment at their previous jobs upon their return home. Whatever it takes to make those serving "whole" financially must be done. We should not ever ask our citizens to serve their country and return from service to find themselves in a bankruptcy.

For those who have sustained injury in combat, the government must be obligated to ensure the best possible aftercare money can buy. The current VA hospital system must be expanded to ensure that all who need care get it. This can be tied in to the education initiative, where government-sponsored medical students, upon completion of their studies, are required to staff these facilities to augment the existing staff.

An area that I feel strongly about is the capabilities of our foreign and domestic spy agencies. The CIA and the FBI are our country's first line of defense against terrorism. Though the FBI is not exactly a spy agency, it is best positioned to deal with counterintelligence within our borders. We have witnessed the poor showing of our counterintelligence agencies before, during, and immediately after 9/11. If we were up to the task, perhaps the terrorist attack of 9/11 would not have happened, and perhaps the intelligence that led us to attack Iraq would have been better, in which case, we may not have undertaken such a grave endeavor. What I am suggesting is that our intelligence agencies need to be strengthened to a far greater degree than exists today. I think that we have begun to rely to a very high degree upon the technological advances of the last few years to derive our intelligence, and that has been our downfall. We need to refill the ranks of the CIA with real spies who specialize in the ways of tradecraft — boots on the ground. I believe we have lost touch with what is going on inside the countries of the world. I no longer believe that we have people who speak the languages or comprehend the cultures of many countries. We can only look at satellite pictures and assume that we know what is really going on. We need to know much more to formulate effective policy.

Technology is a wonderful thing, but I'm afraid that in too many cases it only increases the speed with which we make poor decisions. Budgets should be expanded to rebuild a strong national and domestic security system. Our collection of national and domestic intelligence and law enforcement agencies must work together, seamlessly sharing data, resources, personnel training, acquisition, and vetting to provide the protection every citizen deserves. A great model to emulate is the Iowa Fusion Center run by Russell Porter. It links the state and local authorities. I believe that it or like systems have been implemented in as many as 48 states. If this can be tied into the federal level, then we would be well on our way to a top-notch security intelligence system.

There is also the issue of the government eavesdropping on cell phone calls. This is also a highly controversial matter, and allowing such activity leads us down a slippery slope. Just how much power are we to concede to our government in the name of national security? This is a matter best left to our courts and elected officials who create the legislation that governs this matter. Personally, I believe that if our security forces (the CIA, FBI, and local law enforcement agencies) deem it appropriate for certain individuals' calls to be monitored, then I am all for it. If there is just cause to believe that monitoring conversations would lead to detecting threats to our security, then, with appropriate safeguards against invasion of privacy, I rule this action reasonable. I do not see where law-abiding citizens have anything to fear.

Chapter 13

Homeland Security

"Government's first duty is to protect the people, not run their lives."

—Ronald Reagan

T raditionally, America has had the luxury of open borders, with minimal security measures in place to deter border crossing. We have, for the most part, welcomed visitors from abroad and did not track their whereabouts while they stayed in this country. Let's face it, for years we looked the other way as migrant workers wandered through this country harvesting our fresh fruits and vegetables. This was never really an issue until 9/11. We were very complacent thinking that our national security services — CIA for foreign and FBI for domestic — would protect us from any threat to our safety. 9/11 proved just how misguided we were. The post 9/11 analysis was shocking in what it revealed. Our intelligence services had actually uncovered a good many pieces of a puzzle that manifested itself as the terrorist attack of 9/11. Some of the pieces we knew well in advance; some we knew days afterwards. Some were known to the CIA, some by the FBI, some by local law enforcement, but none by all!

A system of intelligence services that seemed to function very well from World War II until 9/11 proved deficient. By law, the CIA and FBI were forbidden to share information. Neither agency shared with local law enforcement unless it absolutely had to. Each agency's systems were designed to serve its own agency and none of them interfaced with any other agency's systems. The individual puzzle pieces known by each of the agencies were siloed, and didn't mean enough to raise suspicions to a high enough level. If all the puzzle pieces were laid out, the dots could probably have been connected.

National Registry

Our laws, and the Constitution upon which our laws are based, are there to guarantee the citizen's protection from an overzealous government. Our liberty and freedom, civil rights, and privacy are our birthright, and our elected officials and appointed judges are the guardians who ensure that citizens are protected from the government that issued that guarantee. Our focus has always been directed to the domestic, meaning that the laws were intended for application within our country. I am sure that we never intended to extend those rights to terrorists within our country's borders. Today, we are faced with a whole new paradigm and a conundrum at that. These same rights that we established to protect citizens of this country are now being applied to noncitizens, mainly illegal immigrants and terrorists. To some extent, this is an admirable extension of our beliefs that all people should be protected when they are in this country. But I don't believe illegal immigrants and terrorists should be entitled to the same liberties guaranteed to citizens by our Constitution.

This is new territory for us as a nation. Our safety and sovereignty are jeopardized when people are allowed to live within our borders illegally, with reasons and whereabouts we know little of. We must, for our own good, implement a national registry governed by a uniform national identification system. This may sound a little like Big Brother, which scares the hell out of many people. This may be the case, but it IS the best way to ensure that our citizens are afforded the protections of our government, because it is also the only way that noncitizens can be tracked and identified.

If we had a comprehensive database that contained the minimum data attributes about ourselves and the maximum data attributes about foreign visitors and temporary workers in this country, we could easily discern the validity of someone's right to be here. If upon entry to this country, all passport information in addition to answers to a specific questionnaire were to be stored in the database, we could easily screen entry and exit. Upon entry, a temporary identification card could be issued and, as a requisite for exit, the card would need to be surrendered. The ID card could be required as additional validation necessary to book travel domestically. This would help our security agencies to track the whereabouts of visitors while in our country. An automated process could be put in place to track the departure and arrival dates of visitors and could also identify those who have violated their length of stay. All law enforcement agencies in the country would have online access to this database. Use of this during routine traffic stops or during arrests could alert authorities to people who are here illegally. I do not feel that this would infringe upon the rights of law-abiding citizens, and the benefits derived would far outweigh any violation of privacy. We have become a target of terrorists and we need to do whatever it entails to protect ourselves from this threat.

United States Coast Guard

As the protector of our shores, the United States Coast Guard is our immediate line of defense against foreign intrusion along our coasts and waterways. The Coast Guard is tasked with many responsibilities, ranging from paramilitary operations to search and rescue. If you live near the coast as I do, you are acutely aware of the reductions in force and bases that the Coast Guard is faced with each budgetary cycle. For search and rescue operations alone, they constantly fight a losing battle. Each year, more Coast Guard Stations are slated to close due to budget cuts. The force is required to cover ever-greater geographical areas with fewer resources. Effectiveness suffers and eventually, despite the valiant efforts put forth by this service, a preventable tragedy will inevitably occur. The Coast Guard's ever-expanding responsibilities include search and rescue, vessel inspection and documentation, buoy maintenance, harbor/coastal protection, and drug/smuggling enforcement and interdiction, to name a few.

Two key paramilitary responsibilities that need maximum funding are port/harbor protection and drug traffic interdiction. The United States is probably one of the world's largest importers of products. As such, we also have many commercial ports of entry. Typically, these ports are located in close proximity to our largest cities, all of which are densely populated. The most common method of transoceanic shipping of products is by way of container, and every port is fully equipped to handle this method of loading and unloading. Trucks are dispatched by the thousands daily to all parts of the country from these ports of entry. There is no question that terrorists view the logistics of this means of transport as an ideal opportunity to launch a devastating terrorist attack upon this country.

One likely attack scenario takes the form of a nuclear device, secreted in a container or ship and detonated upon arrival at a port. The nuclear device could be a dirty bomb, which when triggered releases highly radioactive material across wide geographic areas. Or, it could be the type used in Japan in World War II, causing widespread destruction and radioactive sickness. Deployment of either type of bomb would be catastrophic. A second likely attack scenario could come in the form of a biological device.

Whatever the impact on the normal flow of commerce, implementation of detection devices and procedures is a must. A detection success rate of 99.9% is failure. Otherwise, oops...there goes New York City, Long Island, southern Connecticut, Westchester, and northern New Jersey. Offshore prescreening and possibly unloading for transfer to regional distribution centers located far from the major centers of population might have to become reality. The Coast Guard, with backup from the U.S. Navy, needs to be fully equipped to take on this most important task of Homeland Security.

Drug smuggling, while not as immediately dramatic as a nuclear or biologic device, is just as catastrophic, only it takes longer to work its evil. Interdiction of drug smugglers pays huge dividends over extended periods of time. There is a three-part solution to this major problem: (1) working with the producing countries to eliminate the production, (2) interdicting the transporters, and (3) delivering strict penalties via our justice system to dealers and users. The Coast Guard, with the help of our Armed Forces, should be ruthless in the apprehension and prosecution of drug smugglers. Drug use by our youth has become far too prevalent at an ever-earlier age. Our country's future is being snorted, smoked, popped, and injected into a wasteland of terrible consequence. Parents are too busy working their lives away to even be aware of just what is transpiring in their children's lives. The drug culture has invaded our homes. The glorification of drugs and their easy availability coupled with peer pressure is often just too tempting for our children to pass up. We need to make drug smugglers cognizant of the fact that we see it to be a deadly business, enough so that the threat of detection by the Coast Guard is enough of a deterrent.

The Coast Guard can no longer be relegated to the back seat of security forces — it needs to be beefed up and brought on par with all other services.

Department of Homeland Security (Airport and Port Security)

The security screening processes at airports vary greatly from airport to airport. I suggest the procedures be made more standard and comprehensive with the constant integration of advanced technologies. These new technologies should minimally include databases for passenger screening, video based software for profiling, and human pattern recognition. This should not only be done upon entry to flights, but also upon exit.

FEMA

Another segment of Homeland Security that is a critical lynchpin for tying the resources of the federal government to the organic agencies at the state and local levels is FEMA. The acronym stands for Federal Emergency Management Agency, and the agency name is a good descriptor of just what it should do: manage emergencies. We all know FEMA from the days of Katrina. Unfortunately, I feel this agency was much maligned for its response to Katrina. The press unjustly placed the blame for inadequate response to that disaster squarely on the shoulders of FEMA. There is no doubt in my mind that FEMA could have responded much better than it did, but there was more than enough blame to spread at the state, city, and parish level as well. There was a total collapse of leadership, command decisions, organization, and response at the local levels, levels that were much closer to identifying what was necessary to prevent disaster. The role of FEMA should have been to coordinate the "heavy lifting" of resources to be distributed as necessary at the local levels. There was no leadership or any organization at the local level for FEMA officials to interface with. There was only chaos.

FEMA should act as the manager and expediter of resources and planning. The basic goal in times of emergency is to connect with local officials who have already begun implementing their localized plans, and identify local needs that FEMA can meet by drawing upon the resources of the federal government, including the National Guard and Army Corp of Engineers. FEMA should not be expected to be the first responder on the scene, because that has to be the responsibility of local level. Rather, FEMA should follow up within a matter of days with the heavy lift that the local levels cannot provide.

Lastly, for those of you who are old enough to remember it, I strongly recommend the reestablishment of a Civil Defense Corps whose purpose would be to organize support response at the most basic levels, providing transportation to and from shelters, distribution and inventory of medical supplies, emergency equipment, and food and water at the community level. This corps would liaise directly with charitable organizations such as the American Red Cross. It should be modeled after the Iowa Fusion Center and tied directly into county and state disaster emergency planning. This is the logical connection point for FEMA to intervene, organizing, transporting, and distributing prepositioned materials using a combination of military and commercially available assets to locally mobilized National Guard units at the state level for further distribution. For cases where personnel evacuation is required, simply reverse the plan.

Recent events, natural disasters, and terror-related incidents have demonstrated the need for and importance of rapid response. Organization and preparedness at the most local of levels coordinated with increasingly higher levels of government will serve to limit panic and casualties, and guarantee a better outcome or chance of survival for all.

Chapter 14

Healthcare

"I predict future happiness for Americans if they can prevent the government from wasting the labors of the people under the pretense of taking care of them."

—Thomas Jefferson

L et me start off this topic by telling you that we in America have the access to some of best medical care anywhere in the world, or that money can buy. That money can buy — that is the rub. It's expensive. We all know it, and every election a new crop of politicians proudly proclaims that they have the answer and will fix the "healthcare for all" issue. With each election, anyone who tries to fix it becomes mired in the pit of partisan politics. Bill Clinton was the smartest; he let Hillary take the lead...and the loss. George W. threw it out for bipartisan consideration and it went nowhere. Obamacare was a truly partisan effort that has been forced down the throats of a populace of which the majority wanted no part. Although there are a few good changes that the legislation correctly identified as necessary, most of the bill should be scrapped and started over.

If you really wanted action on this issue, I had a stupid, and sadly, probably effective suggestion. Mandate that as of the beginning of the next term of Congress, all federal employees, past, present and future, will no longer receive their old Gold plated healthcare benefits. Instead they will be given the option to sign on to a mediocre HMO plan and pay the same copays, deductibles, and contributions that the average worker in private enterprise is faced with. Or they can purchase their own plan out of pocket. When, and only when, the elected officials design and implement a healthcare plan that satisfies **cost, service, availability, and affordability (for both federal government budget purposes and subscriber wallet purposes)**, will the federal employees be allowed to switch plans (to the new plan only). Anybody want to take bets that this wouldn't be the first order of business for the new Congress? I didn't think so!

Let's examine some of the factors enveloping this volatile issue. First of all there are the healthcare insurers. These are the companies we love to hate. We hate them for a whole host of reasons — high cost of premiums, copays, deductibles, authorizations, inadequate networks, and uninspired customer service. We love them only in time of real need. We detest them when they dare to show a profit and when they annually raise our premiums!

I spent ten years employed by healthcare insurers, so I have some insight into their functioning. Like all other insurance companies, they are a risk-based business. Simply put, if they underestimate the risk and have to pay out claims worth more than they take in, in premium dollars, they are unprofitable. After all, these companies are in the business of making a profit. They are companies just like the ones you work for. They are corporations that are in a thankless lose-lose position most of the time. Members hate them for all the reasons stated above and providers (doctors) hate them because they never get paid the amount they bill for. The doctors feel they are always being nickeled and dimed to death by the healthcare insurers. The fact is that both the insured and the doctors are right! But, unlike some other major corporations whose earnings reports blow you away by their enormous profits, the health insurers for the most part never show enormous profits and most often are barely or reasonably profitable.

I have worked closely with actuaries and underwriters to statistically determine claims tables that are used as the basis for forecasting payouts. These in turn are used to determine premiums. Simplistically speaking, aside from productivity gains or unusual occurrences, profits can be based on this methodology. Both the insured and the doctors bitch because of fee schedules that are termed usual and customary. This is what governs the amount an insurance company will likely pay for any given service. Doctors usually charge more than this fee and subscribers paying deductibles have to pay the spread, or some portion between the two. When subscribers have to pay the deductible, they are unhappy; when the deductible is met, the doctors have to accept the usual and customary schedule as final payment if they are part of the health insurer's network. They are not happy with this outcome either. Doctor's practices are a business just like any other. They have costs and expenses that must be offset by revenues so they can make a profit, to which they are justifiably entitled.

Healthcare expenses also emanate from hospitals. From an operations standpoint, hospitals are typically extremely inefficient. Although they are chock full of the latest medical technology, they were extremely slow to adapt cost control technology. They have made great strides over the last few years, but they are not on par with their nonmedical business brethren as far as implementing cost-cutting technology. Hospitals are also faced with another problem that drives up their costs. Whether you have insurance or not, if you go to a hospital, the hospital must treat you. For all too many people, the hospital emergency room is their primary source of medical care. This is a very expensive option for those with insurance, and even more expensive for the hospital treating those without insurance. For those without insurance, this cost to hospitals is either written off as bad debt, charity if the hospital is private, or subsidized by local or state government via taxes. This ongoing problem (uninsured) will persist until all citizens have health insurance coverage.

Part of the problem is the scarcity of doctors, especially in more rural areas. Part of the problem is the reimbursement of providers is too low. Part of the problem is insurance premiums are too high, both for subscriber coverage and for malpractice coverage. Part of the problem is the inefficiency of the infrastructure of the medical delivery system, primarily lack of system automation, but also costly duplication of services within geographic regions. Part of the problem is the costly and inefficient use of hospitals for primary care services, especially the emergency room. Part of the problem is inefficient design, scarcity, and implementation of outpatient satellite clinics. And part of the problem is the use of Medicare fee structures as a basis to implement reasonable and customary payment schedules. Everything is out of whack and everyone tries to game the system to make it work to his or her advantage and, in too many cases, just to survive.

What we have here is a 1,000-horsepower, 24-cylinder engine designed to run on high test, and it is running on four cylinders, producing 90 horsepower running on ethanol. What we really need is a 500-horsepower, six-cylinder engine that runs on regular.

We basically have all the components necessary to provide the world-class healthcare that everyone in this country desires; we only need to tinker with the apparatus to achieve our goal. This is easier said than done, but being the optimistic soul that I am, I believe that the can-do attitude of Americans, added to some negotiation and common sense, will create something we can all be proud of. Here is my plan.

First things first! I am going to borrow a phrase that I believe is Newt Gingrich's. No matter what you may feel about its origins, it is nevertheless most appropriate for this endeavor. We need to have the politicians establish a "Contract with America." Since no one trusts our elected officials to accomplish anything unless there is something in it for them, we will set the table as such. As of the first day of the new Congress, the Cadillac of healthcare plans, which all federal employees receive, becomes null and void and is replaced with a basic Medicare-like plan of coverage. This will remain in effect until the newly reconditioned healthcare delivery system is in place. Then, all federal employees will transition to that plan. Progress on the work in process will be reported to the public weekly with detailed descriptions of accomplishments and snags.

First of all, we need to address the shortage of medical professionals. I propose that the federal government set up a government-funded program to train medical professionals. Careers in medicine, nursing, and medical technologies can be made available to all who qualify. Conditionally, as repayment for the education provided, graduates would be required to commit to internships of a number of years in teaching hospitals, research centers such as NIH and CDC; VA hospitals; rural, underserved clinics and practices; and military units.

Secondly, many medical specialties are underserved, not because of a lack of professionals with the qualifications, but rather a lack of desire. Many physicians have given up practicing high-risk specialties due to the enormous cost burden of malpractice insurance. Is it the insurance companies' fault? No, they are only passing the cost of doing business onto the physicians. The insurance companies provide a service and are entitled to make a reasonable profit from their businesses, too.

So where is the problem? The problem resides with trial lawyers, jury awards, professional medical associations, and incompetent doctors. They all share a portion of the blame. No matter how competent a physician is, when performing a high-risk procedure, there is always the possibility of an unintended and devastating outcome. There are no guarantees of success anywhere. Sooner or later, the probability of an undesirable outcome will prevail, even if the doctor did everything right or everything possible to prevent it. The problem occurs because when a devastating loss occurs, regardless of circumstance, it is only natural to want revenge.

This can be accommodated by a malpractice lawsuit. There are all too many legal eagles out there who are only too happy to facilitate this process, and all too many juries who are sympathetic to the plaintiff, resulting in outrageous monetary awards. This isn't to say that there aren't any malpractice lawsuits with merit; it has just gotten way out of hand. It is just way too easy in our current system to file a malpractice suit against a physician. The consequences of the suits seem to be way too one-sided. If a physician is deemed at fault and the jury awards the plaintiff compensation, the physician's insurance company foots the bill and the physician's insurance coverage cost is increased, or maybe even dropped. The physician either pays higher premiums or switches his specialty to a less risky one, or maybe stops practicing altogether. If the award is deserved, the consequences may be appropriate. If the award is undeserved, the consequences could be devastating. If the jury finds for the defendant, the plaintiff feels wronged and may be responsible for court costs. The physician escapes paying damages, but walks away most likely facing a higher future insurance premium and a stained record.

One way to resolve this issue might be to change the rules of the award based upon the outcome of the verdict. If the physician is found guilty, then along with the current consequences, the American Medical Association and state licensing boards should also be required to rule on the physician's right to continue practice. The AMA and state licensing boards must police their members and licensed practitioners. They may deem the physician to be the victim of unexpected outcome, having followed prescribed and normal safe procedure. In this case, the physician may be allowed to continue practice without risk of a higher insurance premium. If this situation arises more than twice, then his right to practice this specialty must be revoked. If, however, the physician is found to be grossly negligent, then the physician's license to practice must be revoked. The AMA and state licensing boards might also be responsible for damages to some extent. This clearly would provide incentive for oversight.

In a case of a physician found by the jury to be innocent of charges, then the plaintiff should be required to pay to the physician triple the damages the plaintiff was seeking in the original lawsuit. Plaintiff and attorney would share this payment equally. I believe that by implementing these sorts of rules, we would see a drastic decrease in frivolous lawsuits and fewer incompetent physicians. I also think that these same rules governing outcomes should be implemented for all types of lawsuits where compensatory damages are sought, including disbarment for filing frivolous lawsuits. I believe that a drastic decrease in lawsuits would in turn drastically lower the insurance premiums charged, solely based on claims tables experience. This would have a multiplier effect, where savings should be reflected in lower charges for service.

When we talk about how health insurance is obtained in this country as opposed to the rest of the world, we see that we have a unique system. Our health insurance is obtained in various ways. Options to secure insurance are through our employer, through individual purchase, or through the government via social programs such as Medicare and Medicaid. The levels of coverage are all over the board in conjunction with the associated costs for that coverage. There are platinum plans that cover everything (like the federal, state, and local or quasi-governmental employee plans where contributions by the individual are either minimal or nonexistent), and there are bare-bones plans that are of little to no real value, despite their cost. There are supplementary plans to fill in the gaps between acquired plans, and there are government-administered plans targeting all sorts of specific populations, for example, CHIP (Child Health Insurance Plan) coverage for children of families who cannot afford health insurance. And, of course, many people choose to forego insurance, maybe due to cost considerations, or not comprehending the need for insurance, the programs available to them, or how to acquire coverage. Or they may have been denied coverage, or be indifferent about the issue.

Whatever the case on an individual basis, the overall state of our country's hodge-podge health insurance industry needs remedy. For a truly comprehensive system of coverage, these factors need addressing: cost, coverage, availability, eligibility, portability, and infrastructure. These factors are intertwined and have contributed to the evolution of our state of affairs.

Let's start with some basic premises. To ensure that all United States citizens are covered for healthcare, we need to establish a national healthcare plan. This does not mean that the federal government becomes the payor or the insurer of all healthcare coverage (the federal government would make a costly, inefficient mess of such responsibilities), it simply means that there is a plan to ensure that all citizens have healthcare coverage.

The first and foremost factor associated with healthcare coverage is COST. There are too many mitigating details that are input to this factor to address them all, but the main and most challenging can be addressed. First of all, medical care is expensive — we all understand that. Some of the reasons are very valid (education, infrastructure, salaries), and some are not (waste, fraud, inefficiency). To address this factor, a number of things can be done.

A baseline of cost and expenses for service needs to be established for profitability margins to be determined. Once margins are established, competition and efficiency (essential to a healthy marketplace) will take effect and act as cost controls. When I worked in the industry, the federal government, via Medicare, based payments for inpatient services on a system called DRGs (Diagnostic Related Groups). DRGs represented a grouping of all services related to treating a particular diagnosis. A specific dollar amount was associated with each DRG, and this was the standard Medicare payment for treatment of that DRG. Take that a step further and create a set of EOCs (Episode of Care), where all services required for treatment of an episode are grouped together for the same purpose that DRGs are used. For instance, a DRG would represent the services required to treat a compound fracture, and an EOC would include all follow-up and rehabilitation services.

This is a simplified example, but the medical industry can surely flesh this out as a comprehensive system of groupings for payment purposes. The same process should be undertaken to address outpatient procedure services. These services can be indexed by geographic region and standard metropolitan areas of statistical reference to adjust for cost differentials. The entire cost and service structure should be under continuous review to account for changes in treatment regimens, technology advances, and cost of living increases. This Medicare fee schedule then would become the underlying baseline for determining the usual and customary rates for payment purposes for the National Health Plan. (This may in part already be in place, if things haven't changed since I left the industry, but if it is still in place, it may require some tinkering to derive a consensus.)

Once a base payment system is in place, there are other opportunities for lowering the cost of healthcare. If everyone has access to healthcare, it should be mandatory that all be required to get periodic physicals. Preventive care is a much less costly option than dealing with a disease or condition after it has manifested itself and requires treatment in an emergency room. If you fail to get your annual physical, your premium should be increased.

After having established a fee schedule, it now becomes a different story to determine how much each and every person is charged for health insurance. In the absence of insurance it would be simple to determine payments for service. This is called pay as you go — if you do not use any service, you pay nothing, but if you have a heart transplant, that is a different story. That is called catastrophic, because the costs associated with the services for such an episode of care are far more than the average person could possibly afford. That is why we have insurance, to make those situations affordable.

There are several methodologies that insurers employ to determine one's cost of premium. Insurers make use of what are termed risk pools; they can be classified as high, low, large, or small, to name a few. They can also establish premiums by experience rating, a method where an entire year's claims for a particular group are accumulated. Throw in reserves, profit, and administrative costs divided by the number of subscribers, and you get the premium amount for each subscriber. Using the pool method, take a statistically significant universe of subscribers and their associated claims, coupled with the size of the pool and the risk associated with each pool (younger people usually require fewer and less costly services than older people), plus the demographic makeup of the pool, and you can accurately predict what the cost of service will be for the pool. Again, this is a simplification of the methodology, but suffice it to say, larger pools are usually less costly to insure than smaller pools, because the risk is spread out over a larger universe of subscribers.

If we were to take the entire population of the country and treat that universe as a large pool, statistically we would spread out the cost and amount of service per individual. If the claims experience were available for this universe, we could accurately predict the number of claims by type and cost. This would make it easy to develop a premium. Absent the actual claims experience, it can still be accomplished with a high degree of accuracy. This is in fact what I propose to do to establish a base premium for the National Health Plan. This would serve as the base plan that every citizen would be required to be enrolled in. It would eliminate the need for portability or COBRA, because you would never be disenrolled from it.

How would we pay for this?

We need to understand that this is a base plan and that other options and private plans are still available through an opt-out — purchasing a private plan offered by independent insurers. The only eligibility requirement for this base plan is that you are a citizen of the United States. You can never be denied coverage. Premiums would be paid in several ways. First, all employers of all sizes, including the self-employed, would be required to pay 50% for the base plan for their employees. The premium would be a wholly deductible business expense. Employers would also be allowed to offer private plans to fully replace or supplement the base plan, but only the cost of a base plan would be fully deductible. The base plan would eliminate deductibles and copays. Employees would be required to contribute a maximum of 50% toward the base plan cost, and the employer would be required to contribute the balance of, or if they choose, the entire premium.

Those enrolled in Medicare or Medicaid (eligibility to be determined) would pay nothing. Coverage for these programs would be the base plan. For Medicaid enrollees, the individual states would still have to come up with a funding mechanism (I suggest one that mimics the Healthcare Trust Fund). Senior citizens (age 65 or older, automatically enrolled in Medicare) should not have to worry about bearing the cost of healthcare after having contributed to Medicare taxes all their working lives. They should not be subject to spending their retirement savings on healthcare. That should be the responsibility of the federal government and a benefit of being a citizen of the United States. This would be the role of the Healthcare Trust Fund, as mentioned in the chapter on Social Security. The Medicare payroll tax would still be in force and a portion of that tax could be earmarked as seed money for the Healthcare Trust Fund.

Where appropriate, I propose that the unemployed and those receiving welfare distributions be enrolled in an educational program to train them how to do medical records transcribing. Medical transcription is an absolute necessity to develop an electronic medical records database. From the standpoint of efficiency, a patient's complete medical history can be accessed and assessed at any point of care. I believe that this alone would greatly increase the efficiency of care, eliminating duplication of unnecessary tests (and costs), and provide a comprehensive history on which to base a better diagnosis and course of future care. For physicians and medical facilities to be eligible to treat any patient with base plan coverage, there would be a requirement to participate in the Electronic Medical Records Database initiative. This database will greatly facilitate the development of National Health Plan premiums, research and development by medical technology corporations such as drug companies, and provide a rich source of data to be mined by the NIH (National Institute of Health) and the CDC (Centers for Disease Control).

Infrastructure is another key component to efficient delivery of medical services. This country is truly blessed with an abundance of excellent medical facilities, staffed with world-class medical professionals. We also have an uneven distribution of specialties within geographic regions. In the larger cities, we find clusters of different facilities staffed with the same specialties within close proximity, resulting in duplicative services. Normally, one might say that this is a good thing; after all, competition yields competitive pricing. However, this is not necessarily the case in the medical field, where the cost for the same service in different hospitals can be vastly different. Most hospitals provide excellent service, but are terribly inefficient at controlling costs. Antiquated accounting, inventory, and purchasing systems all contribute to irrational pricing and impact bottom line profitability. The Medicare system, the ultimate owner of the National Health Plan, should mandate that for a medical facility to be eligible to participate in the base plan, it must implement a set of software chosen from an approved Medicare vendor list. This software would handle patient registration, receivables, payables, inventory, purchasing, and billing and interface with the electronic medical records database. All applications would also be required to interface with and support standard electronic file transfers via established standards. This would go a long way in reducing waste, establishing cost controls, producing accurate financial reporting, and, last but not least, in helping to prevent the fraud and abuse that is rampant in the current Medicare system.

Infrastructure also plays a major role in accessibility to services. Though, as stated previously, we find duplicated medical services in the larger cities, we find fewer specialties to support the local populations in the suburbs and rural areas. I propose that the Medicare system, in conjunction with the professional medical associations, develop standards that prescribe the appropriate mix of services and facilities necessary to support reasonable accessibility to all the population in all geographic regions. I believe that poorly serviced regions are prone to more severe illness because they lack preventive care. If it is too far to go to see a medical professional, by the time a patient feels sick enough to make the effort, the malady is probably too late to treat cost-effectively. The infrastructure and staffing of suburban and rural facilities to support accessibility can be accomplished in the following ways.

For private healthcare enterprises to be granted licenses and certifications to deliver healthcare services within a geographic area, they must also submit a plan that demonstrates their commitment and ability to service suburban and satellite clinics. Medical professionals who have received governmental support for their education would be required to staff these facilities as part of their contractual agreement. If private enterprise is either unwilling or there is no private enterprise available to provide service, then state and local municipalities could be allowed to participate and receive financial support from the federal government via the Medicare system. In the densely populated cities, the appropriate mix of services by hospital within geographic areas needs to be assessed and aligned with need. This is necessary to eliminate duplicate and unnecessary services, thereby helping to also reduce costs.

The United States government should function as the provider of absolute last resort. Safety nets exist at all levels of government to provide for the needs of the uninsured. Government may help in the formulation of policy to direct and match those without coverage to providers of insurance. The last thing we need in this country is a national universal healthcare plan. Time and again, the U.S. government has demonstrated that it is the least efficient and least likely entity to carry out this role.

The cost of brand-name prescription drugs is the bane of the current Medicare program. As I understand it, the cost associated with the research and development of new drugs is enormous. For drug manufacturers to successfully bring to market new drugs, they must be assured that they can recoup their costs and reap a reasonable profit before their patent protection runs out. Once a patent runs out, other manufacturers are able to produce generic versions of these drugs at a much lower cost, creating a scenario where the brand- name profits are drastically reduced. To attain the goals of the drug manufacturers while still under patent protection, the cost of brand-name drugs is necessarily expensive.

What I propose to rectify this situation could be a win/win for all involved. If the lifetime of a patent for new drugs was extended, say doubled, the drug companies could be assured of goal attainment, albeit over a longer time period. In exchange for this extension of patent lifetime, brand-name drugs prescribed via the national health plan would be obtained at a sizable discount from today's pricing structure. This in effect would lower the cost to the government and consumer, spreading the cost over twice the time period, while still allowing the drug manufacturers to attain profitability. This would in effect provide drug companies the incentive to keep developing new drugs and not be so pressured to immediately recoup their development costs. Think about it.

As I said initially, we in this great country of ours have the best medical care available anywhere in the world. The delivery system just needs a bit of tweaking to make it efficient, affordable, accessible, and profitable for all. I believe I have laid out some groundwork for making that possible.

Chapter 15

Foreign Relations (Policy) and the United Nations

"The days of 'traditional values' and strong foreign policy are over."

—**Chuck Schumer**

D uring the relatively short time that our country has been in existence, we have been involved in 11 major wars with foreign countries, including the War of Independence, our conflict with the British in the War of 1812, the Spanish American War, World War I, World War II, the Korean War, the Vietnam War, Desert Storm with Iraq, Iraq again, and Afghanistan. We have also been involved in other conflicts of minor extent and duration. We were also involved in a Cold War with the Soviet Union. Generally speaking, we have entered these conflicts either because we have been drawn in as allies to friendly countries that have been attacked (World War I, World War II, Korea, Desert Storm), or have (depending upon your opinion) correctly or incorrectly intervened in places of our own choice. We have invested untold amounts of "blood and treasure" on behalf of many nations, including ours.

Before World War I, we were an isolationist nation with no desire whatsoever to become entwined in the hostilities of Europe. Overnight, the European continent exploded, Germany was on the verge of defeating both France and Britain, and the sinking of the passenger liner

Lusitania by German boats, among other things, caused us to enter the war on the side of the Allies. With our help, on the 11th hour of the 11th day of the 11th month of 1918, an armistice was signed ending World War I. Germany was defeated, and France and Britain remained sovereign nations.

But, the Treaty of Versailles, which officially ended the shooting, was an ineffective disgrace that only led to victor reparation resentment and hostilities and, furthermore, set the stage for World War II. World War I was supposed to be the "War to End All Wars." It wasn't. Woodrow Wilson introduced the League of Nations in an attempt to provide a venue for the nations of the world to peacefully resolve issues and disputes. It, too, was a disaster, since no one was interested in resolving disputes peacefully (or maybe the location of San Francisco just wasn't glamorous enough to entice attendance).

History was to repeat itself some 20 short years later, only with a slightly expanded cast of nation states. Neville Chamberlain, Britain's Foreign Secretary, tried to negotiate a treaty of appeasement with Adolph Hitler in an effort to avoid another full-blown war. Hitler smiled, said yes, and continued on with his quest to expand the Fatherland, restore the pride of the German populace, and extract a bit of revenge for the grievances wrought upon the German people as a result of the Treaty of Versailles. Once again, America was drawn into a conflict we wanted no part of (this statement may be subject for debate). Circumstances, mainly the attack on Pearl Harbor and the moral necessity to save our European friends, caused us to enter into the war.

America was the arsenal of Democracy and saved both Britain's and France's bacon once again. Britain always remembered and appreciated our sacrifice, and they became staunch allies. The French let pride get in the way of their collective thinking and forever have been ungrateful. What's more, they took every opportunity to thwart any of our future world policy initiatives. A defeated Germany was smart enough to realize that, without our help, they would be speaking Russian instead of German. They appreciated (to an extent) our presence in their country after World War II during the ensuing Cold War with the Soviet Union. The Russians, who originally sided with Hitler (lest we forget), hadn't counted on their ally (Germany) reneging on their alliance and driving all the way to Moscow. They couldn't wait for us to invade France and open up a second front with Germany. With the advent of VE Day, we were faced with another world menace in the name of Josef Stalin. We battled him and his successors throughout the Cold War in Cuba, Vietnam, Korea, and other remote places around the globe. The arms race between the Soviet Union and us eventually bankrupted the Soviets, as the economics of Communism couldn't match those of capitalism.

China's Communist government is taking a somewhat more pragmatic approach to capitalism, but that doctrine is also headed for eventual failure, as freedom and consumerism will cause either revolution or democracy in the future. Japan, the other major defeated nation of World War II, embraced the Marshall Plan, democracy, and capitalism. They have adapted very well to the competition of the global forum and have remained a "quiet" ally of the United States (their constitution limits their military to homeland defense only).

The United States and the Soviet Union emerged from World War II as the world's super powers. Although their forms of government were direct opposites, these two countries both maintained the military might, muscle, and technical ability to project force, protection, and willpower over their spheres of influence. "Us versus them" translated into "good versus evil." By default, the United States became the world's policeman and whenever countries were in trouble and needed help, we were called in to provide assistance. Britain was no longer

Queen of the Seas, and Britain's colonial empire disintegrated after World War II. France, despite its bluster, was impotent. After World War II, Italy became a military nonfactor, and both Germany and Japan were constitutionally pacifist. China, while immense, was incapable of projecting its military might much beyond its borders.

After World War II, another attempt was made to provide a world forum to peacefully settle the issues of the world. The United Nations was plopped in New York City with much fanfare and hopes that the world would change its way of resolving differences and providing assistance to underdeveloped nations.

While the United Nations proved to be accepted more readily than its predecessor, the League of Nations, it definitely was not to be all that it was supposed to be. From a humanitarian standpoint, it has accomplished much in providing disaster relief, food programs, economic help, and worthy educational programs. The biggest disappointment (and I consider it a failure) was the Security Council. Established after World War II, the "super powers and the victors were anointed with permanent member status with veto power over any and all resolutions. Those five members — the United States, the Soviet Union, China, Great Britain, and France — would forever be adversarial in doctrine and desire. All five members would have to agree upon a resolution for any military enforcement action. This amounted to a preinstalled roadblock to any meaningful action.

Instead, the Security Council provided a soapbox for the five permanent members to endlessly debate one another, accuse one another, and filibuster issues to death without accomplishing anything (sounds just like our Senate and House). It was powerless in its infancy and remains powerless to this day. It has been host to scandal and corruption, and what's worse, the United States (i.e., you and I) foot most of the bill for its operations. It occupies choice real estate in New York

City, its core members have immunity, which they abuse constantly (traffic and parking violations are never paid, costing New York City a fortune every year), it provides safe houses and is a nexus for foreign spies, and, worst of all, resides in our country, in New York City, the capital of the world.

Do we really need it? NO, we do not! The Security Council is a waste of time and humanitarian efforts undertaken by the United Nations always seem to be supplemented by additional U.S. aid anyway. Charitable organizations in the United States also provide far more aid to the rest of the world than do all the rest of the nations of the world combined. It is time for the rest of the world to step up to the plate.

I propose that we relocate the headquarters of the United Nations to a place where it may prove more effective and closer to areas of need, such as Darfur. We should reallocate our budget for the United Nations to help fight poverty in the United States, and, if there is anything left over, add it to our international aid program budget. The real estate that is currently occupied by the United Nations headquarters should be given to New York City as restitution for traffic violations, and at least some of it could be turned into a park.

Conflict within our world seems to be inevitable; the more things change, the more they remain the same. The United States can no longer afford to be the world's policeman without being justly compensated for its efforts. After World War II, we maintained a military presence in a number of countries (Britain, Germany, Japan, the Philippines) and after the Korean War, South Korea. We still maintain a presence in all but the Philippines. Our derived benefit from these presences is an advanced military base(s) from which we can police the world. This is a very heavy cost for the United States taxpayer to bear. It might prove to be even more costly to the host nations and for us if we left. A few years ago, the Philippine government kicked us out of their country. Now that the Cold War is over, Germany is not especially happy about our presence. Both the Japanese and Korean populaces are not in favor of our presence, but their governments are. North Korea still presents a threat to their security. Britain appears to remain as one of our few staunch allies — maybe British memories run deeper than most.

The North Atlantic Treaty Organization (NATO) and the South East Asia Treaty Organization (SEATO) were born to combat the aggressive ambitions of belligerent nations such as the Soviet Union. During the course of the Cold War, NATO proved to be a success in terms of uniting the military of member nations. This was primarily due to the military threat posed by the Soviet Union to member nations. Political philosophies were not usually as in sync, but without the combined NATO forces and especially the contribution of the United States, these member nations could not even begin to resist the Soviet forces by themselves.

After the demise of the Soviet Union, the NATO organization's primary mission no longer existed, though NATO continued to function. The United States began to use NATO more as a political tool than a military one. With the collapse of the Soviet Union, many of the former satellite states of the Soviet Union wanted to become members of NATO, seeking the security of what that organization represented, never wanting to be under the dominance of the Soviets again. If anything, NATO has become an irritating thorn in the side of Russia. Putin views NATO as an instrument the United States uses solely to remind the Russian nation of its demise and Russia clearly treats NATO as a threat to Russian sovereignty. This use of NATO as an extension of our foreign policy is wrong and will only serve to foster ill will and could reignite another Cold War with Russia. This has recently played out in the form of the Georgia/Russian conflict. A renewal of Russian military display of force and an undesirable use of Russian policy are being used to influence and hold hostage those European nations dependant upon Russia for natural gas supplies.

The United States usually commanded the respect of the world's nations, whether our policies were agreeable or not. We haven't always been right, but we were more often right than wrong. During the aftermath of the terrorist attacks of 9/11, the United States was extended the good will of most nations. We could have easily garnered the moral, political, and military support of most of the world in our efforts to combat terrorism. We had it when we retaliated against Afghanistan and its Taliban government that harbored the terrorists. We lost it when we invaded Iraq. We squandered our goodwill and consequently are despised throughout much of the world. We overstepped the bounds of world mandate and have been paying for it ever since. We need to reestablish our moral integrity in the eyes of the world and we need to do it quickly and correctly.

As I see it, foreign policy is a combination of humanitarian, trade, immigration, monetary, and military policy. The United States is the greatest country in the world, and any nation having established friendly relations with us derives great benefits. This should not be taken for granted by our esteemed politicians, friendly nations, nor by not so friendly nations. Usually nation states that are considered our friends benefit enormously from our generosity. One of the most coveted benefits, besides security, is most favored nation trade status. Our economy, in good times and bad, is the most vibrant and safe harbor for conducting world commerce. When economic times are difficult, the United States is the economic system where foreign money parks itself. Our government-backed securities are the most sought after and our economy is the world marketplace in which imports are freely traded with little restriction. Access to this market is the envy of all nations in the world. Our free trade policy is far less restrictive than any of our trading partners the world over.

As such, we as a nation state need to revisit the list of so-called friendly nations we have granted most favored nation trading status to and determine who really is a friend and who is not. The economy of the United States is driven by both imports and exports. Lately, we have been on a down slope as far as exports of manufactured goods are concerned. Many of the products we traditionally manufactured domestically have been outsourced to foreign bases of manufacture. This is not all bad, but our own country has been losing many skilled jobs to these foreign manufacturers. Since our balance of trade is dependent upon the fair exchange of goods, the playing field must be level for all participants. We need not become a protectionist nation, but fair trade must be a condition for the granting and maintaining of most favored nation trade status. If it is determined that our products are restricted in any way from a trading partner's market, then we must seriously consider revoking the most favored nation trading status and immediately halt import of goods from that partner. This is a privilege that is granted and is not a right.

The same sort of policy should be in place for immigration, monetary, humanitarian, and military relationships. The United States taxpayer incurs an enormous tax burden associated with foreign aid of all kinds. It is only fair that the return on investment to the taxpayer remains consistently high. We must establish qualifications and rules that are enforceable in order to allow entry into this highly desirable club called the United States of America.

Chapter 16

Infrastructure: Transportation —
Planes, Trains, Automobiles,
and Boats

"Status quo, you know, is Latin for 'the mess we're in.'"
—Ronald Reagan

D ue to the geographical size of this country, commercial air
travel is a must when traversing coast to coast, and usually
from one city to another. The state of our current commercial
air travel system is at best inconvenient, at worst a nightmare. All too
often, a short haul trip between cities within close proximity of each
other takes longer by air than by car. There are many contributing
factors.

Let's start with the airlines themselves. Until the price of fuel became too prohibitive to support half-full planes, every airline tried to
service every route that its competitors did. Flight departure times for
all airlines tended to cluster around the same times so arrival times at
the final destinations accommodated business travelers, the airlines'
most profitable customers. Since 9/11 and the implementation of
security screening of passengers, these timetables have resulted in utter
chaos for the traveler. Security screening is a long and tedious process
that results in logjams and wasted time. After managing to get through
security, passengers board a plane only to push back from the gate and
sometimes wait for hours on the tarmac or flight line until they finally

take off. On-time arrival at the final destination is purely a hit or miss proposition and never guaranteed; it is an iffy proposition at best.

Why would any sane person want to subject himself to this kind of torture just to fly, for instance, from New York City to Albany, New York? The trip to Albany by car is usually about three hours. The trip to Albany by train is usually about three hours. The trip by air is also about three hours. You might ask how can this be, that all three modes of travel take the same time? A train surely travels faster than a car, and a plane surely travels faster than both a car and a train. The answer is that just to get to an airport takes time; going through security adds more time; boarding, waiting in line to take off, waiting for clearance to land, and waiting for baggage add even more time. Once you have your bags, you must now secure transportation to your intended final destination in Albany. Are we having fun yet? Much the same scenario occurs by train. Even though a car is slower in speed traveled, you still arrive at your final destination at much the same time. What's more, travel by car is the least costly and least inconvenient.

If you were to go back a few years, say to the decades of the 30s, 40s, and 50s, distance travel in this country was most probably by train. There were hundreds of railroad companies serving rural, urban, and intercity travel. The transportation hub of every city was the railroad station. Transfers from rail to auto were easily accomplished by taxi, bus, or private auto. Transit systems were designed to integrate effortlessly to yield an efficient mode of travel. Major railroads were everywhere. Major names such as Santa Fe, Burlington Northern, Pennsylvania Rail Road, New Haven, Jersey Central, Chesapeake Rail Road, Northern Pacific, Southern Pacific, and Illinois Central were but a few that were proud to offer first-class passenger travel between hundreds of cities. Sad to say, most of these have been relegated to the railroad bone yard or are but a shell of what they used to be. The singer

Arlo Guthrie chronicles this in his famous song of lament, "City of New Orleans." The post-World War II era of the 50s witnessed the decline of our nation's proud railroad heritage. Because the rail mode of travel has declined in popularity, the infrastructure and integrated transfer modalities have all fallen into disuse and disrepair. It would take a major initiative with specific objectives to renew this form of transport in an efficient manner.

The Eisenhower administration, with the development of the Eisenhower Interstate Highway System, championed the age of the automobile. The Interstate highway system was developed much in the same vein as the autobahn in Germany, to facilitate transport of military and emergency equipment during times of national crisis. To this day, a very high percentage of public transportation budgets are allocated to the repair and upkeep of this nation's roadways. The primary means of transport for every individual is the automobile. Without the auto, the average American would be immobilized. As a result, our roadways are overcrowded, in terrible shape due to overuse, and unable to handle the daily volume of traffic. This has led to a terrible waste of time and fuel, because we rely so heavily upon the auto for transport to the exclusion of other means.

Air travel entered the equation at the same time as the auto due to the rapid advances in aerospace technology during World War II. Commercial air travel was still pretty much in its infancy and reserved for those who could afford it, but it would quickly grow in leaps and bounds. The rush to develop infrastructure, such as airports, to support this budding industry resulted in serving the then present needs but totally disregarded the future needs. We now have airports close to inner cities without the ability to expand to meet the needs of current day volumes. This results in constant delays, overcrowding, and unacceptably dangerous conditions. For far too long, our airlines have been too unprofitable to support the level of maintenance and infrastructure needed to provide safe and reliable service.

The airlines themselves are not the only part of the air transport industry that is in need of upgrade. A more vital component of the system that is totally behind the scenes is in desperate need of major change. The air traffic control system, on which all air travel depends, is in such disarray and short staffed that at times one wonders how we survive so long without a major disaster.

The FAA is the culprit that is in need of a total reorganization to address the antiquated systems, short staffing, safety guidelines and enforcement, training, and compensation structure of its employees. This agency is a disaster waiting to happen. Unfortunately, when it does happen, it will be at the cost of innocent lives. It will cause major disruptions within the industry for a prolonged time period until the root causes are addressed and rectified. One immediate mandate that the FAA should implement is the inclusion of GPS in the design and manufacture of every airframe that will ultimately fly in United States airspace. Ground control and air traffic control facilities need to have integrated systems that utilize this technology. This needs to be mandated for implementation within a few years and it has to become an FAA regulation immediately.

What we need is a total revamp of our transportation system to sync distance traveled with convenience, safety, and cost. Our current transportation system encompassing all forms of travel in this country is a jumble of bubblegum and piano wire.

I will illustrate just one aspect of sheer stupidity that I encounter on a daily basis. My daily commute consists of a round-trip of 250 miles. I can commute by three different options: Option A: auto/train/shuttle, Option B: auto/ferry/train/shuttle, or Option C: auto.

If I chose to use Option A, I would have to drive to the train station where I would have to pay for parking, buy a monthly commuter ticket on the railroad, transfer to a subway and pay another fare, take a different train line using another monthly train ticket, and finally pay for a taxi to get to work. The total monthly cost would be approximately $900 and take four and a half hours each way.

If I chose Option B, I would have to drive to the ferry terminal where parking would be free (for now); the ferry would require a monthly commuter ticket; I would need to buy a monthly commuter ticket on the railroad; and then finally pay for a taxi to get to work. The total monthly cost would be approximately $700 and take four hours each way.

Option C, driving, requires gas, two bridge tolls, and a thruway toll. The total monthly cost would be approximately $400 and take two hours each way.

While using mass transit, Option A or B, is the environmentally friendly way to commute, it neither saves time nor is cost-effective. Option C, driving is the least expensive, the least time consuming, and the most convenient. I am not tied to schedules that aren't always met and would quite often add additional hours to my commute. While driving is most preferable, I still cannot take advantage of HOV lanes, because I am the only one in my car. There are no other people who could car pool with me due to my destination. Again, while driving is preferable, it is quite often a nightmare. There are a minimum of eight locations along my route where bottlenecks occur and sometimes these result in delays of more than an hour. One particular bottleneck occurs on a four-lane (in each direction) stretch where the road splits to go either to the George Washington Bridge or the Throggs Neck Bridge, which is my destination. This stretch is about four miles. A couple of years ago, while this area was under construction, the road was divided and access to the George Washington Bridge or the Throggs Neck

Bridge was determined at the very beginning of the four-mile stretch. During this period of about a year, I never encountered a tie-up and covered this stretch in about four minutes. Traffic to the George Washington Bridge never seemed to be tied up either. It was wonderful.

As soon as the construction was completed, the barrier was eliminated and traffic immediately came to a dead stop. It would typically take up to an hour to navigate this stretch. Why? Traffic volume was the same. The answer is simply that all four lanes of traffic would try to merge into two at the very end of the stretch. Three quarters of the traffic wanted to go to the George Washington Bridge, and the merging traffic blocked access to the Throggs Neck Bridge. I have often wondered why the Department of Transportation never took notice of why the traffic flowed without incident during construction, and after construction, came to a standstill again. The amount of wasted time and fuel each day is enormous, and for no good reason, other than poor design of traffic patterns. This kind of inefficiency is repeated all over the New York metropolitan area each and every day. I would bet that this lunacy is not limited to New York, but repeated to some degree all over the country in all metropolitan areas. This translates into enormous waste of time and fuel each and every day.

What this country lacks is a comprehensive transportation plan. It seems that each state has a Department of Transportation that serves its own microcosm of needs. It appears that these needs are often recognized, planned for, funded, and implemented with less than total satisfaction. When completed, improvements are often "too little, too late" to satisfy dynamic needs. I suggest that a comprehensive transportation planning commission be established to address all forms of transport at a national level. I also suggest that ideas such as a comprehensive review of integrated modalities of transport be designed to accommodate daily commutation and long- and short-haul passenger and commercial traffic.

There are areas, such as I-95 between Maine and Washington, D.C., that are totally inadequate for our current needs and that can be vastly improved with a little thought. The Connecticut Turnpike, for instance, is a nightmare when heading north in the afternoon. The George Washington Bridge and the Cross Bronx Expressway at any time of day in either direction are a constant nightmare. These routes could certainly benefit from redesign to include multilevel roadways that service limited access commercial only on a particular level, passenger only on other parts, and local access on a third level.

Time of use restrictions by vehicle type could also be incorporated. Since these rights of way are already well-established on all interstates, a form of light rail rapid transit and high-speed passenger service using them could certainly reestablish the use of rail as an efficient means of travel. If efficient rail networks, along with the necessary local connections for transfer to subway, taxi, and shuttle/bus could be developed, rail travel could easily replace short haul air travel. Our rail networks should be redeveloped to serve a bulk of freight movement nationwide. Container ports should be tightly integrated to rail for efficient transport to regional destinations where transfer to truck for final destination would occur.

Elimination of many of the duplicative short-haul airline flights between cities that could be better served by first-class (clean, comfortable, timely, affordable, and safe) rail service should alleviate congestion to a degree where longer-haul service could be profitable. This could happen because fewer flights would have to take off and land within a very confined window. A reinvented FAA with state-of-the-art systems and a reorganized workforce, which is better trained, better paid, and better staffed, would benefit all who travel by air by ensuring better, safer ground control and traffic management. Air travel could once again be efficient, affordable, and safe for the traveler, and profitable for the airline companies.

All forms of transport are valid and efficient in their own right. A comprehensive national transportation plan that wisely integrates all modalities and is futuristic in design will better serve this country's economic, military, and travel needs forever. We simply need to use the right tool for the right job. The current stimulus plan that will supposedly rebuild our nation's infrastructure may be well intentioned, but I fear that we will just be throwing money at problems that will not serve the future comprehensively. Microcosms may benefit to a degree, but we may end up just prolonging the inevitable by propagating existing problems that will never be solved without a comprehensive future master plan.

Boats

When I was a little kid, my father took me into the city every once in a while to see the passenger liners in port. During those trips, we passed by the piers that handled cargo ships. Since my father's work included marine transport, I became familiar with ships of all kinds. I was also afforded the opportunity to get aboard a few of these ships while they were in port. I can remember cargo ships of the American Export Lines, Moore McCormick Lines, and United States Lines. These were cargo ships that traveled around the world and brought back all sorts of goods, at a time when trade flourished. As we drove up along the Hudson River, we could see what appeared to be thousands (but were really hundreds) of tied up, gray-painted liberty ships that had been mothballed. These were all a testament to the wartime Merchant Marine. The liberty ships spoke to a time when shipbuilding capacity in this country was unrivaled. Sadly, those times are long gone. Now, ship building yards, the few that still remain, most often support the construction of our naval military ships. And, it seems these are fewer and fewer.

Most of the merchant cargo ships that ply the oceans are of foreign construction, usually out of the Far East shipyards. So too are the passenger cruise ships that seem to be making a comeback. American shipbuilding is but a ghost of what it was, and so, too, is the steel industry that fed this once thriving segment of our economy.

This just does not sit well with me, as the world has transitioned to a global economy and much of the goods that we purchase are of foreign manufacture. The primary means of transport for this foreign-manufactured merchandise is by boat from China and other Far Eastern countries. America supports free trade. That is a good thing. What is not so good is that most of our imported goods are arriving in this country on ships that are built in overseas shipyards and staffed by foreign crews. We no longer have the wherewithal to supply the transport or crew capacity to carry on this trade. From a commerce standpoint, this is unwise, but from a national security standpoint, it is even worse. Our military, as evidenced by the logistics of the Gulf Wars, depends upon our Merchant Marine for lift capacity to support our troops in foreign lands. If we were ever to become engaged in conflicts that required supply in opposite directions, like during World War II, I am not sure that we could adequately handle the logistics with the existing U.S. Merchant Marine.

There could be a possible solution to both these problems, and its benefits would extend beyond the marine industry. Again, free trade is a good thing, but I believe free trade should be accompanied by fair trade. The manufacture and exchange of goods between countries may constitute free trade, but it cannot stop there. Free trade must be extended to include transport as well. That transport should be minimally carried on at least 50% by our own Merchant Marine: United States-built and crewed vessels. Only then would I consider it to be free and fair trade. The two major benefits obvious from such an arrangement are:

1. The revitalization of a shipbuilding industry and a Merchant Marine industry, along with all the associated industries that support and supply these, such as steel.

2. National security. In time of conflict, the Merchant Marine would be better able to support logistics, shipbuilding facilities would be available for ramped up production if needed, and the steel industry might once again become revitalized and competitive, all necessary to support national security and keep this country safe, secure, and independent.

I will reiterate once again here — regional container ports that are located well outside the inner city harbors should be developed. This is also a long-term project, but the planning for transportation hub links to rail and highway should be started immediately. This aspect of transport will serve to relieve congestion within our major coastal cities/harbors, provide a secure remote location for interdiction of illegal merchandise, provide jobs within both construction and steel industries, and help to make us more self-reliant in times of national crisis.

We all know about the massive stimulus aid package of recent years. The broken record talking points used to justify this package point out that five million people would be put back to work rebuilding our aged and decrepit failing roads and bridges. References were made to the poor maintenance of these transport infrastructure components, implying that once completed during the Eisenhower administration (and beyond), they were disregarded and left to crumble. This kind of rhetoric may sell policy, but it is utter hogwash. This is a typical feel-good knee-jerk reaction to make people think that a solution to our economic dire straits is at hand. The portrayal of a crumbling auto transport infrastructure is simply not true. The federal, state, and local governments spend billions of dollars each year toward the upkeep and new construction of highways, roads, and bridges.

There is no question that more can and should be done, but it should be done intelligently and under the guise of a national security comprehensive master plan. If we are going to speak infrastructure, then we need to take the blinders off and refocus on all aspects of infrastructure, and not simply throw our money at make-work projects, mortgaging our future (no pun intended). While there are countless aspects to infrastructure that can and should be addressed, three that come to the immediate forefront and need attention are our electrical grid, clean water systems, and communications grid. All three would benefit tremendously from improvement, as well as the citizens that depend upon them (all of us).

Electrical Grid

I am not an electrical engineer, so I am not an expert in this area, but I do keep up with current events and am very aware of existing problems with our national electric grid. I believe it was way back in the 60s, when I was a kid, that there was a blackout that covered the entire Northeast. I recall that the cause was a circuit breaker that didn't trip, or something to that effect. It was a ridiculously inexpensive part that caused the entire Northeast to be blacked out for an extensive time period. After the incident, we were assured that it would never happen again, as new and improved safeguards were in place. Well, I seem to recall that there have been multiple blackouts, countless brownouts, and every time there are ice storms and hurricanes, power outages.

I expect that there are many factors that contribute, including the inadequate power- generating capacity. Although these occurrences may seem rare, they are serious, especially where national security is concerned. In times of crisis, electrical power, which we normally take for granted, is essential to the health, safety, and continued normal and emergency operations of our infrastructure, governments, and social systems.

We need to be assured that failure of our national grid is not an option. How can we accomplish this? Once again, there needs to be a comprehensive study where all power providers, inclusive of generation and distribution capabilities, regardless of fuel source, develop a comprehensive master plan to rebuild our grid structure with state-of-the-art technologies designed to be double and triple redundant in nature. Failover without interruption is a must. Too many of our current distribution systems are vintage 1930s technology and are totally exposed to the elements.

One of the greatest threats that we face, albeit an extreme case, is the detonation of a nuclear device smuggled into this country by a terrorist organization. An attack by a sovereign nation using a nuclear device with EMP (electromagnetic pulse) is also in the realm of possibility. Unless we are shielded from this sort of event, we are at risk. A nationwide grid system could be designed to be underground and protected from atmospheric elements that may cause disruption of service. This grid system should be a plug-and-play design with multiple redundancies built in. Super conductive materials should be the foundation to support and increase efficiency of distribution.

Clearly, I am by no means an expert in such matters, but it seems only logical that much needs to be done and that much can be done to ensure that our electrical grid can be upgraded to face today's challenges and those of the future. I believe that this is an area of infrastructure that is of a higher priority than spending massive amounts of money on idiotic pork projects of questionable value.

Clean Water Systems

Another utility that most, but not all, of us across this country take for granted is the clean drinking water that spews forth from our taps. Fortunately for us, there have been few if any national emergencies concerning the availability of clean drinking water. Over the course of time, my lifetime anyway, I have always been aware of drought conditions that seem to happen every decade or so in the Northeast. Since I live in the Northeast, I am more acutely aware of these conditions than what occurs in other parts of the country. Having said that, I have recently been more attuned to these same conditions occurring more frequently, and almost seasonally, across the nation. It does seem that every region of the country has experienced severe water shortages in recent times. Annually, devastating forest fires and wildfires have plagued the Western states and Florida. Drought conditions have contributed greatly to the cause and sustainability of these fires. There is a current debate attributing these seemingly prevailing conditions to global warming (since discredited by author manufactured/rigged data).

Whatever the cause, our conservation measures do not seem to be able to keep up with the demand for clean water. Continued residential and commercial development in regions that depend upon river water as a primary source for drinking water just adds additional stress upon an uncertain supply. This can eventually lead to water wars between all factions of society, such as agriculture, industry, ranching, and residences that depend upon water for life and livelihood. We cannot control the weather to ensure that rainfall replenishes our water supplies, but we can take other actions to ensure clean supplies of drinking water.

Some things that are within reach, but not necessarily substantive in increasing supply, are conservation and pollution control. These are no-brainers, but will definitely serve to enhance sustainability. One thing that we have not been able to do, even with all our technological prowess, is make water. One thing our ancestors before us learned was to capture and save water when it rained during the rainy seasons. Rainfall from roof run-off was channeled and captured in cisterns and barrels for future use when the dry seasons came. To this day, we still do this via reservoirs and dams on our rivers. No matter how much we use these practices to store and conserve water, we are still ultimately dependent upon the weather systems to replenish our supply.

Almost infinite sources of water supply to which we have unlimited access are the oceans that surround our country on three sides, and the Great Lakes on the fourth side. The Great Lakes are a source of basically fresh potable water, while the Gulf of Mexico, Atlantic and Pacific oceans are salt water. As we all know, salt water is not drinkable. However, as many municipalities have already learned, salt water can be converted to drinking water via desalinization. Cities along the coastlines have a ready source of water supply to feed the desalinization plants.

What about cities inland of the coast? This is where investment in infrastructure can play a vital role in securing a safe and abundant source of drinking water. Just as the ancient Romans created a series of aqueducts for transport of water, so can we. This is certainly not a short-term project, but as evidenced by the ten years invested by New York City in building tunnels for the transport of water from upstate reservoirs, it can and should be done. Whether it be that desalinization plants are located on the coasts and fresh water is transported via under/above ground aqueducts to storage facilities throughout the country or vice versa, this project is worthy of consideration. Since most of these desalinization plants would be on or near the coast, and since they require substantial energy to operate, this would be an ideal opportunity to build solar electric generating facilities to support this project. The longer we put off starting a project of this magnitude, the longer we are at the mercy of unexpected and severe drought conditions.

Telecommunication Systems

Americans carry millions of cell phones with us every day. We are dependent upon them and take them for granted. Just take one second to think about how difficult your day is when you leave the house and forget to bring your cell phone. Sure you can survive, but if you are anything like the typical 25-year-old who cannot go ten minutes without texting, calling, taking and sending pictures: life becomes a bore.

On a more serious note, for those of you, like me, who were in New York City during the terrorist attacks of 9/11, the vulnerability of our telecommunications systems is crystal clear. In a matter of seconds, cell phone coverage was wiped out, and when you could get access to a network, it was just like every New Year's Eve at midnight — "at this time, all circuits are busy, please try again later." The telecommunications providers did a splendid job recovering and restoring service, but for those of us who were here, it was pure hell. The hell does not refer to the inconvenience of not having cell service; it refers to the millions of family, friends, and emergency personnel who were absolutely desperate to ascertain the status of people who may or may not have been in the World Trade Center towers. I am sorry to say that time seems to have diminished the magnitude of the tragedy of that day for people outside the geographical locale of New York City. For people within the New York metropolitan area, it will always be in the forefront of our minds.

Having said that and having lived through that experience, I have come to appreciate the vulnerability of the citizens of this country. Communications are vital for any community to survive any sort of calamity that may befall us. Technology has provided us with the ability to nearly instantaneously access people or data with the simple touch or keystroke of a communications device. It is an integral part of our lives. As such, to ensure 100% availability, there needs to be multiple layers of redundancy designed into our communications networks. If our communications satellites become inoperative, landline via fiber or shielded cable must become immediately and transparently operative. Failovers need to be redundant and secure, with the ability to use the most technologically advanced systems, along with the ability to integrate with older technology. All network contingencies should be maintained, upgraded, and system-tested as newer more secure and dependable technology becomes available.

The electric, water, and telecommunications grids/systems, while built and owned by privately owned and operated companies, must be integrated into a master plan governed by the Department of Homeland Security. Although this may appear to be very much along the lines of Big Brother, such a plan for security will never come to fruition without the mandate of the federal government.

Chapter 17

Taxes

"To compel a man to subsidize with his taxes the propagation of ideas which he disbelieves and abhors is sinful and tyrannical."
—Thomas Jefferson

I don't know about you, but taxes are the bane of my existence. Don't get me wrong — I strongly believe that it is my duty and obligation as a citizen of this country to contribute monetarily to its continued functioning via taxes. I also happen to believe that it is the fiduciary responsibility of my elected officials to keep my tax burden to a minimum via balanced budgets using zero-based budgeting with annual increases indexed to the CPI. Having said that, I fear that my utopian dream will never come to fruition until there are radical changes to the composition and ideology of our current crop of elected officials.

I was absolutely appalled by Obama's use of scare tactics to ram through a stimulus bill costing taxpayers almost $800 billion dollars without anyone having reasonable time even to read the proposed legislation. The logic used for the urgent vote and passage of this bill was that it would limit unemployment to 8% and generate minimally 3.5 million new jobs in the areas of construction and green energy production. Well, as of November 2009, unemployment was 10% and all indications are that it will continue to rise or hold steady around 9% in the foreseeable future.

The 3.5 million new jobs have been reduced to "saving" 150,000 jobs, which in all professional opinions is completely unverifiable, and at best amounts to wishful thinking. Before passage, many economics professionals and historians to no avail ruefully pointed to the FDR New Deal programs during the Great Depression that were implemented to remedy that financial crisis as an example of the illogic of this bill. Historically speaking, government stimulus spending does NOT work.

Taxpayer funded bailout via TARP monies for the financial and insurance industries, GM (now "government motors"), and Chrysler have burdened us even further, and that is on top of a massive new budget in the trillions of dollars range. Obama pushed for rapid passage of healthcare reform for the uninsured and cap and trade legislation using the same fear tactics he used for passage of the economic stimulus bill. His logic for passing healthcare reform is that the costs are rising out of control and are contributing to our economic crisis. This is all hogwash of course, and the final outcome will only be to drive competition from the market, limit services, and drive up the costs via taxes for all of us.

Cap and trade, whose purpose is to limit carbon dioxide emissions in order to save the environment, is another massive tax hike on us all. Obama freely admitted that the cost of this program would skyrocket the cost of our energy bills. There is consensus in the scientific community that carbon dioxide emissions are a problem that needs to be addressed. However, with the revelation that the data to support this was fudged, the raw data was deleted, and studies that were contrary to those of proponents of global warming were intentionally suppressed, the urgency to implement CO_2 reductions has diminished.

Furthermore, unless every country in the world signs onto this agreement and strictly enforces it, the playing field for our manufacturing base will become so lopsided that we will become noncompetitive in the global economy due to the enormous costs heaped on industry. Personally, I just don't see countries like Russia, China, India, African nations, Middle Eastern nations, and for that matter, the rest of the world, abiding by these rules. How is this to be verified? We are being played for fools. Who is ultimately going to pay for this? You and I, the taxpayers of course!

Last year, I heard on the news that the chief analyst of the EPA, who is also a scientist, wrote a white paper that disputed the methodologies, data, and conclusions of the global warming position. This position is the basis that the EPA is using for justification of the Obama proposed cap and trade legislation. The Obama-appointed head of the EPA sent this analyst an e-mail (which later was made public), instructing him never to release this white paper because it was contrary to the position that the EPA had taken, and might jeopardize the passage of the cap and trade legislation. So much for trusting our government to not tax us with impunity.

Here is the rub — after paying federal, state, and local taxes, which annually increase at a rate much faster than my income, I now pay almost 50% of my earnings in taxes. I heard reported in the news that 50% of those filing federal tax returns pay no taxes, but receive a tax refund from the government. That means that only 50% of the citizens who file federal tax returns actually pay taxes to the federal government. I personally consider this to be an unfair and disproportional burden placed upon too few of the citizens of this country. Further, the implications for future elections are extremely disturbing. Consider what the future of America would be if politicians campaigned for continued and increasing entitlements. These politicians would be elected. Fewer and fewer people would be incentivized to actually earn a living and pay taxes; instead they would rely upon the federal government for their fiscal livelihood, cradle to grave.

It seems that every time that Congress proposes new legislation that is the least bit controversial because of cost or policy, the Congress decides that the rich will foot the bill. Since only 50% of us actually pay federal taxes, this type of logic will eventually bankrupt all but the smallest percentage of taxpayers in the country. What happens when even the rich run out of enough money to support the country? Where taxation without representation is tyranny, I also believe that representation without taxation is the logical path to socialism. Eventually, private property is relinquished and/or diminished and the state by default becomes the owner of everything. While this is a simplified explanation of the road to socialism, it is nonetheless a path that I believe we are on. Ironically, it is possible because American heritage and policy support it.

If we were to go back in time to the pre-Revolutionary War days of our country, we can begin to understand just what I am saying. The colonists were subjects of King George V. As subjects, they were required to abide by the laws and rules imposed upon them by the king. Some of those laws and restrictions included the mandatory purchase of all manufactured goods from England, and the reciprocal sale of all goods produced by the colonists to England at prices favorable to the crown. The colonists were also required to pay taxes to the crown. While the colonists felt that these actions were unfair, because they received very little benefit in return, they had little recourse. When the tax burdens and restrictions placed upon them by the crown, such as the stamp tax and the purchase of tea from the crown, became too much to bear, the colonists reacted.

Americans historically do not like to pay taxes, nor suffer the inequities from policies dictated to them by leadership whose authority they question. Even during the course of, and post revolution, Americans were not partial to paying taxes to support their own Continental Congress and, later, federal government for the services provided, minimal that they were. Americans were an independent bunch. They wanted little from and sought to give little back to their government. They did not necessarily look with disdain upon the wealthy, nor expect the wealthy to support them. They simply wanted the freedom and opportunity to pursue their own dreams of becoming wealthy. Sadly, that attitude is only partially true today, being most evident in recent immigrants, legal and illegal, who still view America as the land of opportunity. Far too many people today rely upon the government for their support, via entitlements and socially engineered legislation such as welfare, food stamp programs, and Medicaid, to name a few.

As the country has matured, so have the demands of the citizens upon our government at all levels, not for essential services such as police and national defense, but desired services in the form of entitlements. Many of these entitlements, such as Social Security, Medicare, and Worker's Compensation, were legislated with the best intentions. While not necessarily ill-conceived, the underlying funding formulas were poorly thought-out and essentially flawed, because they were not adjusted to compensate for the constant changes to the rules governing the dispersal of these entitlements.

Over time, this resulted in the creation of unsustainable deficits and deficit spending. As America progressed down the path of legislating desires, the humanitarian aspect of our generosity took hold. Social engineering became more and more prominent as a way to ease the monetary burdens of those less fortunate. Legislators on both the federal and state level have even found a way to legislate without assuming the burden of cost through unfunded mandates. These are very popular for those on the receiving end of benefits, and extremely expensive for those footing the bill but not partaking in those benefits. The paradigm has shifted, from wanting little from the Federal Government, to expecting the federal government to take care of all our needs. We are becoming a "nanny" state via legislation.

Unfortunately, the tax burden associated with all this legislation falls on fewer and fewer taxpayers. The governments at all levels are desperate to find sources of tax revenue necessary to support all this legislation. Ultimately, everyone pays some of the freight via payroll taxes, sales taxes, excise taxes, and thousands of other types of usage taxes. The balance of the tax burden is borne by business and individuals.

When we speak of business we naturally think of companies like IBM, Boeing, JP Morgan Chase, and Hewlett Packard, along with all the rest of the Fortune 1000. These are big companies that contribute large amounts to the tax revenue stream. It is also very easy to assume that these big companies can easily bear their tax burdens. What is also very unfortunate is that we fail to clearly distinguish between big and small business. We casually lump them together theoretically for the purpose of taxation. What we fail to sufficiently recognize is that small business represents approximately 65% of all business. More importantly, at least from a tax standpoint, is that small business tax revenues are derived from the filings of individual personal tax returns. Because of this, the owners of small business appear to also be the wealthy. Tax increases on business and the wealthy become a double whammy on small business people. The effect of so much enacted legislation that derives its funding from the wealthy could be disastrous.

I believe that most Americans are more than willing to contribute their fair share of taxes to preserve the union and support social programs that help the less fortunate. I also fear that with fewer and fewer people able to shoulder this tax burden, the resentment of those paying will only increase. Our elected officials need to understand this before the "colonists" once again react. One way the colonists might react is to lower the gross amount of taxable income reported by utilizing a cash or barter system where payments go unreported. This in effect would shrink the taxable base even further. We can no longer afford to keep promoting legislation that rewards people for inaction. With 50% of those who file federal income tax returns paying NO federal taxes, our ability to fund entitlements and socially engineered benefits diminishes.

There are two other negative aspects of such high tax burdens paid by the minority of Americans.

First, every dollar of taxes that business and individuals pay to the government is one less dollar that can be employed by the economy. Business and individuals are the most efficient allocators of resources, while the government is the least efficient. The multiplier effect of private investment is ultimately what drives the economy, and the economy is where tax revenues are derived. The more the government takes, the less vibrant the economy will become. If we continue on this path, we will end up bankrupt.

Second, providing safety nets, such as continuing to extend unemployment paychecks and subsidizing healthcare insurance, welfare benefits, and any other federal or state-subsidized tax credits, provides a disincentive for those on the receiving end to modify their behavior. Those who find themselves unemployed are already dispirited and become more so if their search for gainful employment is not successful. I am not against providing a safety net for those in times of need; I am against the government fostering this as a way of life. There is a better way.

Business in this country is the highest taxed in the world. This puts our domestic companies at a competitive disadvantage right off the bat. It makes it harder to compete in the global and domestic marketplace because high taxes just add to overhead, and overhead has to be added to the cost of a product. If we want to regain competitiveness, we must lower the tax burden on our business.

The individual personal federal, state, and local income tax prepara-
tion is a nightmare for most people. Even some of the most well-
educated and savvy people I know cannot deal with filling out their own
tax returns. Despite innumerable attempts by the IRS and state tax
entities to simplify the process, the system is still too complex with too
many different rules and forms to account for every conceivable option.
It is a wonder that any tax returns are filled out correctly at all.

These are two very good, major, and minor, but different reasons
that our tax system needs to be overhauled.

We are now beginning to hear murmurs of the federal government
wanting to push for a value added tax (VAT) on top of every other tax
already imposed upon us. Why? Because the governments have grossly
over spent and over promised on far too many programs and bureau-
cracies. It is totally unsustainable unless government spending is
curtailed via a balanced budget that respects citizens' own personal
budgets.

There is a simple solution that could be gradually achieved over a
number of years. Implementing a flat tax and drastically cutting the
size of governments at all levels is the most prudent thing that could be
done to revitalize the economy and rebuild America's fiscal health.

We as a country absolutely need to drastically reduce the amount of
tax dollars our elected officials spend on our (or more likely) their
behalf. Our collective goal should be to reduce the federal budget by
minimally 50% within two years, and another 5% per year over the next
four years.

The first thing that needs to be accomplished is a comprehensive
review of every government program that is funded by the federal
government. These need to be classified in multiple ways such as
national security (armed forces, homeland security) and social support
(health, education, and welfare), with designations of criticality —

"critical" ranked a ten, and "nice to have" ranked a one. Anything that falls below a five in national security and anything that falls below an eight in social support should only be a candidate for continued funding if tax revenues permit.

Nice to haves — for example, national, state, and local parks — should be candidates for management by subcontracting, as is already done in some states like Arizona. RFPs should be let out for bidding where the bidding entity pays a fee to the government and in turn runs the parks according to established guidelines. Reasonable entry fees and concession income would be the source of all revenues for the contractor.

The federal payroll should be immediately trimmed by 50%, either by a reduction in head count and/or renegotiation of salaries and benefits. The elimination of nonessential government programs will help in this regard. In no case, should government salaries and benefits exceed the equivalent of those in the private sector. An analysis by *USA TODAY* published 8/10/2010 found that federal civil servants earned average pay and benefits of $123,049 in 2009, as opposed to $61,051 for those in the private sector. The disparity can be attributed to automatic annual increases in salary and benefits for the government sector, while private sector increases are most often subject to the state of the economy, enterprise profitability, and gains in productivity. Federal workers seem to be immune to these harsh realities. This is clearly demonstrated as President Obama has requested a 1.4% across-the-board pay increase for 2011. In addition, seniority pay increases would also be applicable. Those of us in the real world who pay for these increases via taxes are very rarely compensated under such generous guidelines. It is more likely that we do things the old-fashioned way: we earn it! Since pension and benefit costs of public sector worker retirees is one of the biggest line items of governments at all levels, the following should be implemented.

Any new public sector hire must not receive a pension. Pensions should be replaced with 401(k)s or other self-funded retirement plans. The governments may contribute a match of x percent indexed to the cost of living, along the lines of private industry.

Existing pension plans must be adjusted to match reality also. Many plans are based upon the last year or so of work. Employees pad their last year with incredible amounts of overtime to build up their salary upon which their pension payout is based. This places an extraordinary burden on future budgets that the taxpayers must fund. In many cases, public employees can retire after twenty years of service with full benefits regardless of their age. Many go on to second careers, sometimes in the public sector, double dipping in the pension system.

I would propose the following, which I feel is a more equitable system for the taxpayers.

After twenty years of service, an employee may retire at any time. After throwing out the three years of lowest salary and the three years of greatest salary, the pension would be based upon the average salary of the remaining years. The employee is fully vested in that pension; however, the employee cannot begin to draw upon that pension until he/she attains the age of 65. During the time between retiring and drawing the pension, the retiree will no longer be eligible to receive health or other benefits; they end with retirement. If the employee chooses to continue employment after twenty years of service, benefits continue until retirement. This would be more in line with private industry, improve budget forecasting, and greatly ease the burden on taxpayers.

Entitlement and social support programs such as unemployment and welfare should require all recipients of benefits to perform a minimum amount of government service, such as roadside (environmental) cleanup, facilities maintenance, census work, etc., in return for benefits.

Those incarcerated in federal prisons should be required to support themselves and the entire cost of the facility. This is already being accomplished in state facilities in Florida (via agricultural programs) and Arizona (via animal shelters). There is no reason why inmates cannot be put into prison programs, such as plant nurseries, farms, and other self- supporting, business-like atmospheres. This would provide the inmates with a rehabilitation program, cost the taxpayers little or nothing, and greatly benefit society as a whole.

The above examples are but a few innovative ways that can be implemented to reduce the cost of government programs and the tax burden on our fellow citizens. We cannot just continue to fund programs with our hard-earned tax dollars without at least a break-even on our investment.

The tax burden place upon the citizenry of this country needs to be equitable and shared by every individual. Noncontributory entitlements, such as the federal earned-income credit, need to be eliminated. Entitlements that foster irresponsibility and provide a disincentive to be productive are a detriment to our society's continued well-being. Every existing entitlement program should be evaluated to determine what the beneficiary can contribute in return for their receiving benefits. All such entitlements should have a clearly defined plan to transition the beneficiary out of the program and become self-sufficient by a mandated sunset date. Everyone needs to have skin in the game. The incentive to achieve must never be eliminated, and those that achieve honestly should never be penalized for doing so. I believe that implementation of a flat tax would be the fairest way for everyone to compete and be rewarded equally.

State and local governments could be allocated a percentage of the revenue derived from the federal income tax returns based upon where each taxpayer resides. This formula would help state and local governments to plan their budgets accordingly and result in fiscally prudent budgets.

Something must be done to stop the irresponsible tax and spend policies of our federal government. We as a nation are currently on a collision course with monetary disaster. I am not foolish enough to pretend that these ideas are the be-all and end-all solution to our fiscal problems. Rather, they are a starting place for prudent dialogue. Taxation without representation is tyranny; representation with reasonable taxation to support a balanced budget is good government!

Epilogue

"Surround yourself with the best people you can find, delegate authority, and don't interfere as long as the policy you've decided upon is being carried out."

—**Ronald Reagan**

I started to write this book about ten years ago. As you probably determined after reading this, many topics are prominent issues at this current time. This is not just a rehash of already covered issues. Ten years ago, I identified these as some of the most important policies/issues to address to keep the U.S. place as world leader. You may or may not agree with my observations or suggested possible solutions, but I have thrown out what I consider to be common sense solutions. I am not an expert. What I am is a proud, but concerned citizen of this country and my only desire is to keep this country as strong as possible.

I have not been even remotely satisfied with the actions of our elected officials. We have let petty, partisan politics rule the day, effectively preventing meaningful legislation from being enacted. We no longer are surprised when scandal, corruption, deceit, or improprieties of any kind are linked to our elected officials. We have come to expect this. Is it any wonder that Congress received the lowest approval rating in this nation's history?

In a recently released poll, Senate majority leader Harry rated a 7% strong approval rating, while Nancy Pelosi, Speaker of the House received a mind-blowing 2% strong approval rating! This has to change. I put aside my skepticism that our newly inaugurated President Barack Obama would follow through with his "change" and reach across the aisle to eliminate partisanship and work with Republicans to effect legislation that benefits all citizens. During the first week of his administration, he failed to rein in Nancy Pelosi who has a vendetta against Republicans.

Obama has reversed interrogation rules, and is closing Gitmo without a plan to relocate the prisoners. Late on a Friday afternoon, when media coverage was lax, he restored funding to Planned Parenthood for abortion services. He stated that he will pass a stimulus package put together by the Democrats, and will not even consider Republican objections, Why? His reason? Because "I won." Regardless of what your positions are on these issues, there were 57 million people who did not vote for Obama. Just because Obama won, it doesn't mean he has the mandate to disregard the wishes of almost half of those who voted. That is pure arrogance and I believe ultimately a foolish and self-destructive mentality. These are highly explosive policies. These actions certainly fail to instill my trust in him. My skepticism is fully restored and not so slowly building ever more.

Politics in this country have become way too divisive. I have toyed with the idea of creating a new party, a New American Party, based upon common sense, honesty, integrity, character, and love of country. This would be a party that encompasses the bulk of mainstream America and is based upon common sense. The party would not seek to satisfy 100% of the population on all issues. That would be nearly impossible. Rather it would seek to satisfy 80% of the populace about 75% of the time. There is a common ground that unites Americans, and that common ground is no longer being served by the current political party system. I believe that until such time as this occurs, we are destined to continue our slide toward irrelevance. I thought that I might be onto something when I heard former New York City Mayor Ed Koch during his weekly radio show on Bloomberg Radio posit much the same thought. How am I doing, Mayor Koch?

Below, as an example of how this New American Party would be representative of all, I have suggested some candidates to fill some positions. At first blush you may wonder what would ever compel me to select this collection of personalities. Over time, each has demonstrated the ability to put forth well-thought-out ideas that would strengthen our country. I do not necessarily agree with all their ideas, but they certainly are pragmatic and sincere. These are all people who know how to lead and get the job done, and that is exactly what our country needs if we are to remain a bastion of freedom and prosperity.

Finally, the whole purpose of this venture is to demonstrate that there are alternative, common-sense approaches to our problems and to identify issues that I feel need to be addressed post-haste. You may not agree with my ideas, but if they serve to initiate debate and eventual resolution, then this collection of thoughts and ideas will have served its purpose.

The New American Party Cabinet Choices

Colin Powell or Lt. Col. Allen West — Secretary of Defense
Rudy Guiliani — Department of Homeland Security
Sen. Fred Thompson (former)
Newt Gingrich — Secretary of State
Joseph Lieberman
Charles Krauthammer
Frank Gaffney
Judd Gregg — Congressional Budget Office
John Bolton
J.C. Watts
Lawrence Kudlow — Secretary of the Treasury

Tom Keane — Federal Reserve Chairman

Charles Paine — Secretary of Commerce

Juan Williams

Mike Huckabee

Dennis Miller — White House Press Secretary

Pat Buchanan

Christiane Amanpour

Pat Caddell

Tom Souzzi

Steven Forbes

Lou Dobbs

Rick Santorum

Stewart Varney

Michael Reagan

Dr. Michael Savage — Ambassador to the United Kingdom

Made in United States
North Haven, CT
31 October 2022

26154403R00124